READING DETECTIVE® Rx

USING HIGHER-ORDER THINKING TO IMPROVE READING COMPREHENSION

Reading Detective® products available in print, software, or eBook form.

Reading Detective® Series
Beginning • A1 • B1 • R$_x$
Math Detective® Series
Beginning • A1 • B1
Science Detective® Series
Beginning • A1
U.S. History Detective® Series
Book 1 • Book 2
World History Detective® Series

Written by
Cheryl Block, Christine Broz,
Margaret Hockett, and David White

Pen and Ink Illustrations by
Susan Giacometti

© 2002
THE CRITICAL THINKING CO.™
www.CriticalThinking.com
Phone: 800-458-4849 • Fax: 541-756-1758
1991 Sherman Ave., Suite 200 • North Bend • OR 97459
ISBN 978-0-89455-801-6

MIX
Paper from responsible sources
FSC® C011935

TABLE OF CONTENTS

Select stories were written by Mary-Ann Lucido and Tom Bentley.

Thank you to the following field-testers:
Edith Hauver, Vanguard Preparatory School, Dallas, TX;
Debi Inman, Mountain Empire Jr./Sr. High, Pine Valley, CA.;
Margaret Ryan, Pitt County Schools, Greenville, N.C.;
Jenny Milton, Briarwood School, Houston, TX;
Cindi Kinney, Homeschooler, Sacramento, CA.

Some images used herein were obtained from IMSI's MasterClips® Premium Image Collection, 1895 Francisco Blvd. East, San Rafael, CA 94901-5506, USA.

TEACHER OVERVIEW

The purpose of this book is to provide instruction and practice in using higher order thinking to develop reading comprehension. The comprehension skills meet state reading standards for secondary students Grades 6+; the reading level is 3rd–5th grade.

The goal of the program is to teach students how to analyze what they read. Students answer questions based on a passage and then provide supporting evidence from the text for their answers. Each sentence is identified with a superscripted number; each paragraph has a letter. Students use these numbers and letters to cite specific sentences and paragraphs as evidence.

The purpose in asking for evidence is to:

- Encourage students to go beyond simple recall of information.
- Require students to support their answers by drawing on specific information from the passage.
- Clarify for the teacher a student's understanding of the material.
- Require students to analyze the passage in greater depth.

Contents

Pre- and posttests offer a general assessment of students' skills before and after using the program. One fiction and one nonfiction passage are offered for each. These tests are NOT intended as a formal diagnostic tool to assess a student's reading abilities. They are simply meant to give you a general idea of your students' skills in reading comprehension. They should be used to determine which skills to focus on.

The book is divided into 11 units: main idea, conclusion/inference, story elements, literary devices, theme, vocabulary, figurative language, cause/effect, prediction, fact/opinion, and mixed skills. Each unit begins with a lesson and practice activity. These lessons are most effective when done with the students. The last unit is a review of all the skills in the book. The skills matrix on page vi breaks down the skills only for the pre- and posttests, Story Elements unit, and mixed skills section. Questions in the other units focus only on one specific skill.

There are three types of reading passages:

- nonfiction articles on a variety of topics in the different content areas
- fictional stories in a variety of writing styles
- literature excerpts from award-winning and well-known authors

Each exercise provides a passage for the student to read followed by a series of questions. Most of the questions are multiple choice or short answer.

A key component in this book is discussion. Some answers include explanations which show how the evidence given supports the correct answer. These explanations can be used as a basis for discussion of students' answer choices and supporting evidence. Many of the questions (inference and prediction, for example) are open to interpretation. It is important to discuss with students how they came up with their answers and how the evidence does or does not support their answers. We give what we consider to be the best possible answers based on the evidence. If you feel a student has made a good case for a response, you can accept that answer. The key to this program is encouraging students to think about what they read in order to better understand it. The evidence that a student gives is the key to pinpointing his or her understanding of the content.

SKILLS FOR READING COMPREHENSION/LITERARY ANALYSIS GRADES

READING COMPREHENSION SKILLS

Skill	Fiction pretest	Nonfiction pretest	12. He's Got Mail	13. Boat People	14. Cross Country	15. A Run Through the Park	16. Face on the Milk Carton	17. The Pink Umbrella	18. Out in the Cold	38. Sing Down the Moon	39. Swim for Your Life	40. The Last Will	41. The Working Child	42. Owls in the Family	43. Tiger Woods	44. Geocaching	Fiction Posttest	Nonfiction Posttest
Cause/Effect	■	■								■	■		■	■			■	■
Compare/Contrast																		
Define Vocabulary in Context	■	■									■		■		■	■	■	
Draw Conclusions		■		■			■						■	■		■	■	
Fact/Opinion		■											■		■	■		■
Identify Author's Purpose																		
Inferences	■	■			■	■			■	■		■		■	■	■	■	■
Main Idea/Supporting Details		■								■			■		■	■		■
Predictions	■										■							■
Reading for Detail		■				■												
Summarize Information					■													
LITERARY ANALYSIS																		
Character/Analyze Traits	■		■	■	■	■	■	■	■		■	■		■			■	
Crisis/Resolution	■		■		■			■			■			■				
Figurative Language	■	■						■				■		■			■	
Literary Devices							■	■	■			■						
Mood/Tone								■		■	■							
Plot/Key Events/Problem	■		■		■	■		■		■				■			■	
Point of View	■				■		■	■						■	■			
Predict Outcome														■			■	
Recognize Conflict			■	■		■		■	■		■	■					■	
Sequence of Events	■					■				■								
Setting	■		■	■	■		■		■	■								
Theme	■										■	■					■	

PRETEST	STORY ELEMENTS/LITERARY DEVICES	MIXED SKILLS — POSTTEST

HOW TO BE A READING DETECTIVE

Reading for Evidence

As you answer the questions, you may be asked for evidence. This evidence is the sentence or paragraph that supports your answer. Always look for the best evidence. In each story, every sentence is numbered and every paragraph begins with a letter. When a question asks for evidence, write the number of the sentence or the letter of the paragraph letter that helped you find the right answer. Read the paragraph below then answer the question.

A ¹Cattle-raising on the African savannas is affecting nature's balance. ²The African savanna, or grassland, is home to asome of Africa's largest animals, such as the elephant and the giraffe. ³A savanna is fairly dry with few trees and plants. ⁴The native animals have learned to share this limited plant life by eating at different levels. ⁵Tall animals eat the tree leaves while smaller animals eat the shrubs and grass. ⁶The native animals leave the new shoots to sprout again. ⁷Cattle are destroying the grasslands because they eat all of the grass, including the new growth.

1. You can conclude that if the new growth is gone, the plants

   A. will take longer to grow.

   B. will not grow back.

   C. will not be affected.

   D. will grow elsewhere.

Which two sentences are the best evidence? ____, ____

Explain how the evidence supports your answer.

_____

_____

_____

Fiction Pretest: The Runaway
by Christine Broz

A [1]The young chocolate Labrador lay on the floor watching her owner's every move. [2]She could sense that something different was about to happen. [3]Tim Brown was packing his belongings to put into storage. [4]He had been ordered to leave immediately for a war being fought half a world away.

B [5]Tim had talked a reluctant friend into giving the dog a home. [6]So the dog moved to the friend's house. [7]The dog was scared and lonely at this new house. [8]The first day, she saw her reflection in a mirror and thought it was a scary looking dog. [9]She started chewing on the corners of the rug and the furniture. [10]Tim's friend was very angry and yelled at her when he returned home each day and discovered her destruction.

C [11]On the third day the dog thought, "Anything is better than this." [12]When she was let out into the yard, she escaped over the back fence. [13]She wandered the streets of the neighborhood all day. [14]Nothing looked familiar to her. [15]Other dogs barked at her from behind fences and windows. [16]Cars blared their horns at her. [17]From time to time, she would see the same white truck with bars on the windows. [18]Her head hung down, and her tail was low between her legs as a result of her fear. [19]The dog thought, "Anything is better than this."

D [20]Finally, a friendly looking woman came to pet her. [21]The woman put her on a leash and led her to the white truck with bars. [22]The lab was taken to an animal shelter full of barking and growling dogs. [23]She was put in a cold cement pen, alone. [24]The dog thought, "Anything is better than this." [25]But there was no chance of escaping this time. [26]Seven long days and nights passed.

E [27]Then a family appeared at the door of her pen. [28]Their faces sparkled with big smiles. [29]The dog's tail began to wag for the first time in a week. [30]They fell in love with her and decided to adopt her. [31]They called her Mocha because her coat was as rich and brown as chocolate. [32]She soon found her place in the warm loving family and thought, "*This* is better than anything."

DIRECTIONS: Circle the letter next to the correct answer or write the answer on the lines given. When asked for evidence, write the number of the sentence or the letter of the paragraph that best supports the answer.

1. What is the theme of the story?
   A. A dog is a man's best friend.
   B. Dogs can adapt to anything.
   C. You can learn from your mistakes.
   D. Sometimes things get worse before they get better.

2. In sentence 5, what does the word *reluctant* mean?
   A. unable
   B. unwilling
   C. unlucky
   D. unhappy

   Which words are a context clue?

   _____

3. The story takes place in:
   A. a city.
   B. a park.
   C. the country.
   D. the wilderness.

   Which sentence is the best evidence? _____

4. What can you infer the dog did because she was lonely and scared in paragraph B?

   _____

   _____

   Which sentence is the best evidence? _____

5. What caused the dog to put her tail between her legs when she was walking the streets?

   _____

   What words in sentence 18 are a clue? _____

6. Put the following events in order.
   ___ Dog is taken to animal shelter.
   ___ Dog is adopted by family.
   ___ Dog is unhappy and escapes.
   ___ Dog's owner goes away and leaves her with a friend.
   ___ Dog is unhappy and can't escape.

7. The story reaches a crisis when the dog:
   A. loses her owner.
   B. goes to the friend's house.
   C. is lost in the neighborhood.
   D. is taken to the shelter.

   Which two sentences are the best evidence? _____, _____

8. Which sentence in paragraph E contains a simile?

   Sentence _____

   Write the simile.

   _____

   _____

9. From whose point of view is the story told?

    A. the friend's
    B. the dog's
    C. Tim's
    D. the new owner's

10. Which sentence in paragraph C foreshadows the dog ending up in the shelter?

    Sentence ____

11. Do you think the dog will try to escape from her new home? Explain the answer.

    _____

    _____

    Which sentence is the best evidence? ____

Nonfiction Pretest: Teen Sleep
by Christine Broz

A [1]Many teens today are sleep deprived. [2]With early start times for schools, increased homework, and afterschool activities cutting into their sleep time, it is no wonder teens feel stressed and tired. [3]But there may be more to it than that!

B [4]Studies show that teens need nine to ten hours of sleep per night in order to be alert the next day. [5]This is more than what they needed when they were younger. [6]Children's internal body clock appears to shift as they become teens. [7]This clock tells them to stay up later at night and get up later in the morning. [8]Along with the change in their body clock, teens' schedules get busier. [9]So, it is quite common for a teen to get an insufficient amount of sleep. [10]Many teens actually get less than eight hours of sleep a night.

C [11]Being sleep deprived has many negative effects on teens. [12]Many teens get poor grades because they are not alert or because they are falling asleep at school. [13]Their brains can be "foggy" until noon or even later. [14]They can become irritable, anxious, or depressed. [15]This can lead to behavioral problems. [16]Teens are more likely to make bad choices and give in to peer pressure when they are tired. [17]The effects of being tired can even be fatal when a sleep-deprived teen gets behind the wheel of a car.

[18]According to the National Highway Safety Administration, drowsiness and fatigue cause more than 100,000 traffic accidents each year, and young drivers are at the wheel in more than half of these crashes.

D [19]Some schools are adjusting their schedules to help solve the problem of teen sleep. [20]Middle and high schools are pushing back their start times from 7:45 to 8:30 in the morning so teens get more time in the morning to sleep. [21]One school has even gone to a 2:30 to 9:00 P.M. schedule to be sure teens are awake during class. [22]Other schools regularly rotate class schedules so that a student doesn't always have the same first period class every day.

E [23]Both teens and adults need to be aware of the need for teens to get enough sleep on a regular basis. [24]This can only help teens thrive and survive those tough adolescent years.

DIRECTIONS: Circle the letter next to the correct answer or write the answer on the lines given. When asked for evidence, write the number of the sentence or the letter of the paragraph that best supports the answer.

1. What is the main idea of the article?
   A. Children and teens have different sleep needs.
   B. Teens have busy schedules.
   C. Teens need to get more sleep.
   D. Some schools adjust their schedules for teens.

2. What does the word *insufficient* mean in sentence 9?
   A. adequate
   B. not enough
   C. too great
   D. interrupted

   Which other sentence gives a context clue? _____

3. In sentence 13, what does the phrase *brains can be "foggy"* mean?

   _____

   _____

4. The topic sentence of paragraph B is _____.

5. Why do some schools have later start times?

   _____

   _____

   Which sentence is the best evidence? _____

6. From paragraph C, you could infer that:
   A. people cannot think or act as well when they are tired.
   B. teens prefer afterschool activities or jobs to school.
   C. schools starting later will solve teens' problems.
   D. people should get at least ten hours of sleep at night.

7. Paragraph D supports the conclusion that:
   A. some schools are attempting to meet students' needs.
   B. schools are making students improve their sleep habits.
   C. school hours are getting longer.
   D. school schedules don't need change.

8. Label the following statements with F for fact or O for opinion.
   ___ Being sleep deprived has negative effects on teens.
   ___ Teens need nine to ten hours of sleep each night.
   ___ The adolescent years are tough.

9. List one of the negative effects of being sleep deprived.

   _____

   _____

IDENTIFYING MAIN IDEA AND SUPPORTING DETAILS

Finding the Main Idea

A nonfiction article has a topic and a main idea. The **topic** tells you what the article is about, such as cooking or pioneer life. The **main idea** tells you what the author wants to say about the topic. An article usually has only one main idea. Read the following article.

A ¹Spiders are not insects. ²They belong to the same class of animals as insects. ³However, there are many differences between spiders and insects.

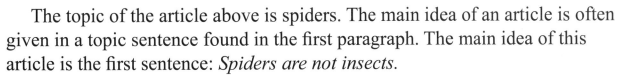

B ⁴The bodies of spiders and insects are different. ⁵A spider's body has two main parts. ⁶The front part is the head and chest together. ⁷The second part is the stomach, or abdomen. ⁸The insect's body has three parts. ⁹In the insect, the head and chest are two separate parts. ¹⁰The abdomen is the third part.

C ¹¹There are other differences between a spider and an insect. ¹²An insect has six legs. ¹³A spider has eight legs. ¹⁴Most insects also have wings and spiders don't. ¹⁵An insect has antennae on its head. ¹⁶A spider has no antennae.

The topic of the article above is spiders. The main idea of an article is often given in a topic sentence found in the first paragraph. The main idea of this article is the first sentence: *Spiders are not insects.*

Each paragraph in an article supports the main idea of the article. For instance, paragraph B explains one reason why spiders are not insects. Each paragraph also has its own topic sentence with a main idea. The **topic sentence** gives the main idea of the paragraph and is usually the first sentence of the paragraph. Sentence 4, the topic sentence of paragraph B, states the main idea that *spiders and insects have different bodies.* The other sentences in the paragraph give **supporting details** that further explain the main idea. In paragraph B, the supporting details describe how the bodies are different.

1. What is the topic sentence in paragraph C? ____

Sometimes the topic sentence of a paragraph is not the first sentence. Read the following paragraph.

D ¹Phan put his last bag in the school recycling bin. ²It took them all day, but they had almost 500 cans. ³They collected more cans than any other group. ⁴Phan and his friends won the school prize for recycling.

2. Which sentence is the topic sentence? _____

The graphic organizer on page 9 can be used to identify the main idea and supporting details of an article or a paragraph. Decide the topic first. Then find the main idea, what the article or paragraph is saying about the topic. You will most likely find it in the first paragraph or the first sentence. The topic sentence of each paragraph following the first paragraph can be given as a supporting detail for an article. The sentences within the paragraph are the supporting details for the paragraph.

MAIN IDEA AND SUPPORTING DETAILS

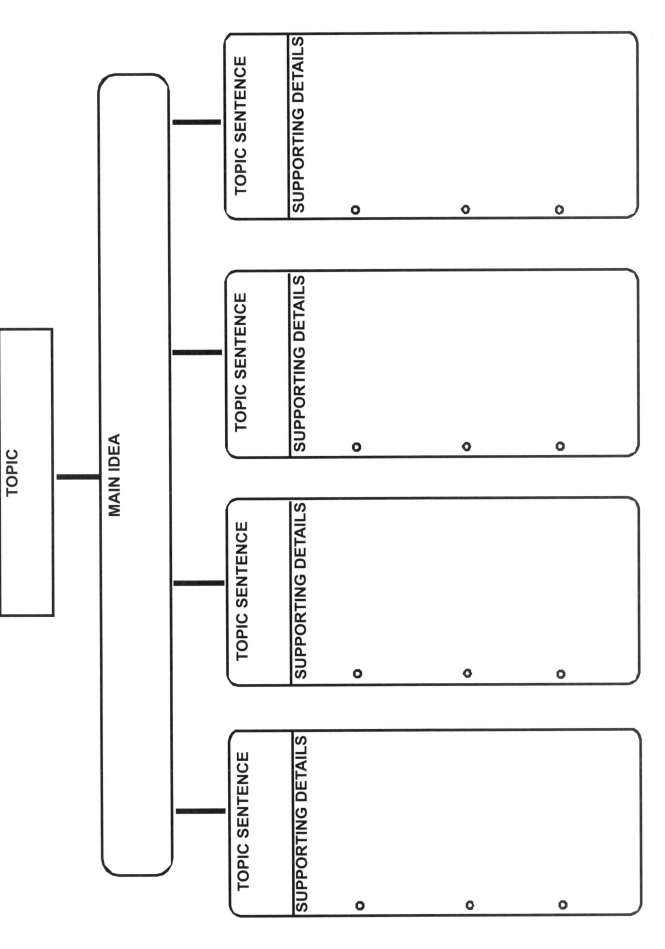

TOPIC

MAIN IDEA

TOPIC SENTENCE

SUPPORTING DETAILS

TOPIC SENTENCE

SUPPORTING DETAILS

TOPIC SENTENCE

SUPPORTING DETAILS

TOPIC SENTENCE

SUPPORTING DETAILS

MAIN IDEA PRACTICE ACTIVITY

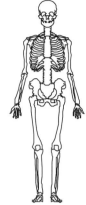

Read the following story.

A ^{1}Imagine what it would be like if you didn't have any bones. ^{2}Your body would be soft and limp. ^{3}Your skeleton is the framework that supports and protects your body.

B ^{4}One important job of the skeleton is to hold the muscles that help your body move. ^{5}The bones provide a place for the muscles to attach. ^{6}Bones are connected by movable joints. ^{7}The muscles allow these joints to move. ^{8}Just like the hinge on a door, the joint does not move by itself. ^{9}It is the push and pull of the muscle that allows the joint to bend and causes movement.

C ^{10}Another job of the skeleton is to protect organs inside your body. ^{11}The skull protects your brain from injury. ^{12}Ribs form a cage to protect your heart and lungs. ^{13}Your skeleton is one of the most important parts of your body.

Complete the main idea graphic organizer. Answering the following questions can help you.

1. What is the main idea of the story?

    A. The skeleton is the framework that supports and protects the body.

    B. The skeleton is connected by joints.

    C. One important job of the skeleton is to hold the muscles that help your body move.

    D. The skull protects the brain from injury.

2. What is the main idea of paragraph B?

A. Joints do not move by themselves.

B. The muscles allow the joints to bend.

C. The skeleton holds the muscles.

D. Joints are a kind of hinge.

Which sentence is the best evidence? ___

3. Which of the following sentences is NOT a supporting detail of paragraph B?

A. Bones provide a place for muscles to attach.

B. Muscles allow joints to move.

C. Joints, like hinges, do not move by themselves.

D. Muscles are part of the skeleton.

4. How does paragraph C support the main idea of the story?

_____

_____

1. Pass the Salt
by Christine Broz

A [1]What comes from water but makes you thirsty? [2]Salt. [3]You may think those tiny crystals are no big deal. [4]However, salt has been one of the most valuable minerals in the history of man.

B [5]The human body needs salt to survive. [6]Salt helps send nerve signals to and from the brain. [7]Salt helps nutrients move around the body. [8]It helps muscles work properly, and it aids digestion.

C [9]In ancient times, you could not buy salt at the local store. [10]People found it near coastal areas where ocean water evaporated and left salt deposits on the ground or underground. [11]It was also found in the meat of animals and fish. [12]Many of the first cities began in areas where there was a natural supply of salt.

D [13]Salt allowed people to keep food longer. [14]It was used to preserve meat, fish, and vegetables so they could be stored and eaten later. [15]Storing food made it possible for large groups of people to survive. [16]The stored-up food kept them from starving during a poor harvest. [17]Some of the foods we eat today—such as sausage, cheese, olives, corned beef, and soy sauce—were invented long ago by using lots of salt.

E [18]Salt was so precious in some areas that it was used like money to trade goods and services. [19]Marco Polo, the explorer, noted the importance of the salt trade routes that crossed China. [20]In Tibet, he saw tiny pressed cakes of salt used as coins. [21]Greek slave traders traded salt for slaves. [22]African traders crossed the Sahara Desert to trade salt for gold. [23]Roman soldiers were even paid with salt. [24]This is where the word *salary* comes from.

F [25]At different times in history, people had to pay the government a tax on salt. [26]These salt taxes paid for wars and built empires. [27]As early as 2200 B.C., a Chinese emperor taxed salt. [28]The British empire was supported by a salt tax. [29]Napoleon brought back the salt tax after the French Revolution to pay for his European wars. [30]The Erie Canal in New York was paid for in part by a salt tax.

G [31]The value of salt is often taken for granted, just as the water we drink and the air we breathe. [32]But without salt, we could not live.

DIRECTIONS: Circle the letter next to the correct answer or write the answer on the lines given. When asked for evidence, write the number of the sentence or the letter of the paragraph that best supports the answer.

1. Which of the following is the main idea of the story?
   A. Salt was not always easy to find.
   B. Salt was used as money to trade goods and services.
   C. Salt has been valuable to man throughout history.
   D. Salt makes you thirsty.

2. What is the main idea of paragraph B?

   _____

   _____

3. What is the main idea of paragraph C?
   A. Salt used to be scarce.
   B. People built villages near salt.
   C. People found salt in nature.
   D. Salt is found in fish and animal meat.

   Which two sentences are the best evidence? ____, ____

4. Sentence 17 supports the main idea of paragraph D that
   A. salt made food taste better.
   B. salt preserved food for storage.
   C. salt could be preserved.
   D. salt made food more valuable.

5. How does paragraph E best support the idea that salt was very valuable to people in the past? It tells
   A. where salt is found.
   B. that salt is found in the Sahara Desert.
   C. where the word salary comes from.
   D. how salt was used as money.

6. Which sentence is the topic sentence in paragraph F?

   Sentence ____

2. Day of Infamy
from Ginger's Diary, 1941

The following entries are taken from the journal of a seventeen-year-old American girl living at Hickam Field, Hawaii, when Pearl Harbor was bombed. The writing is reproduced as originally written, in the style of a diary—with short comments and incomplete sentences.

Saturday, December 6, 1941

A [1]Washed my hair finally. [2]It's warm again, so it dried real fast. [3]Read the paper and then it was time to eat lunch. [4]Listened to the Shriner's football game over the radio. [5]The University beat Willamette 20 – 6. [6]I spent all afternoon reading funny books and trying to get our transportation figured out for tonight. [7]Finally fixed it so Hester took us, and Dad brought us home. [8]We (Kay and I) were ushering at Punahou for the play "Mr and Mrs. North." [9]It was pretty good. [10]We got home about ten of twelve and I'm very sleepy. [11]Lani invited us to dinner Tuesday.

Sunday, December 7, 1941

B [12]BOMBED! [13]8:00 in the morning. [14]Unknown attacker so far! [15]Pearl Harbor in flames! [16]Also Hickam hangar line. [17]So far no houses bombed here.

C [18]5 of 11:00. [19]We've left the post. [20]It got too hot. [21]The PX is in flames, also the barracks. [22]We made a dash during a lull. [23]Left everything we own there.... [24]A couple of non-com's houses demolished. [25]Hope Kay is O.K. [26]We're at M's. [27]It's all so sudden and surprising I can't believe it's really happening. [28]It's awful. [29]School is discontinued until further notice...there goes my graduation.

D [30]Shortwave: Direct hit on barracks, 350 killed. [31]Wonder if I knew any of them. [32]Been quiet all afternoon. [33]Left Bill on duty at the U. [34]Blackout all night of course!

DIRECTIONS: Circle the letter next to the correct answer or write the answer on the lines given. When asked for evidence, write the number of the sentence or the letter of the paragraph that best supports the answer.

1. About what time of day did the author probably write in her journal on Saturday?
   A. 8:00 A.M.
   B. noon
   C. midafternoon
   D. midnight

   Which sentence is the best evidence? _____

2. Which is the main idea of paragraph B?
   A. BOMBED!
   B. Pearl Harbor in flames!
   C. Unknown attacker so far!
   D. 8:00 in the morning.

   How does sentence 15 support the main idea?

   _____

   _____

3. Sentence 21 supports the main idea of paragraph C that:
   A. the weather was too hot.
   B. they had to leave the post.
   C. the PX and barracks are on fire.
   D. school is being discontinued.

   Which sentence is the topic sentence? _____

4. Which sentence in paragraph C supports the idea that the writer is a high school senior?

   Sentence _____

5. How many were killed when the barracks were hit?

   _____

6. Which sentences support the idea that Saturday was a day much like any other Saturday?
   A. 3, 4, 6
   B. 12, 13, 14
   C. 7, 8, 9
   D. 9, 10, 11

3. A Breed Apart
by Cheryl Block

A [1]Search and rescue dogs are carefully selected and trained to find and save people in many different situations. [2]They find hikers lost in the wilderness. [3]They rescue swimmers and boaters from lakes and rivers. [4]Disaster dogs find and rescue people after major events such as floods and earthquakes. [5]One of the earliest uses of these dogs was finding people buried by avalanches. [6]Dogs are now being used to look for people after manmade disasters, such as the attack on the World Trade Center.

B [7]Dogs can be trained to identify specific scents. [8]They have a much better sense of smell than humans. [9]An item belonging to a missing person is given to a dog to help it recognize that person's scent from others. [10]Dogs used in water rescue can even pick up a person's scent from the air. [11]Disaster dogs must be trained not only to identify live human scent but also to ignore all other smells. [12]They save firefighters precious time in finding live victims buried below.

C [13]A search and rescue dog must have three traits. [14]It needs lots of energy. [15]It must be fearless and willing to face danger with its handler. [16]It must also have a strong prey drive, which is a dog's instinct to hunt. [17]Rescue dogs often come from animal shelters. [18]The traits that make good search dogs do not make these dogs good family pets.

NDSDF FEMA-certified dog *Billy* with Mike & Scott at the World Trade Center, 11/01.

D [19]Dogs are trained for different kinds of search and rescue. [20]A dog tracking a lost hiker uses different skills than a dog involved in a water rescue. [21]Dogs used in water rescues are trained to work from a boat and to bite at the water to alert the rescuer of a victim. [22]Disaster dogs receive FEMA* training from the NDSDF*. [23]They learn to walk on uneven surfaces so they will not lose their balance when searching huge piles of rubble. [24]They must crawl into small openings and through dark tunnels.

E [25]Search and rescue dogs risk their lives to save others. [26]They seem to sense their important role and will work tirelessly. [27]A dog can become so focused on its task that it won't even stop for water. [28]Dogs hooked up to IVs for fluids were a common sight at the World Trade Center disaster. [29]Search and rescue dogs will keep going until the job is done. [30]They have found people in remote areas and pulled victims from the rubble of buildings. [31]They are truly man's best friends.

*FEMA: Federal Emergency Management Agency
**NDSDF: National Disaster Search Dog Foundation

DIRECTIONS: Circle the letter next to the correct answer or write the answer on the lines given. When asked for evidence, write the number of the sentence or the letter of the paragraph that best supports the answer.

1. What is the main idea of the article?
   A. Rescue dogs risk their lives to save others.
   B. Dogs must have certain traits to be a good search and rescue dog.
   C. Dogs are carefully trained to find people.
   D. Dogs are chosen and trained for many different types of rescue.

2. What is the main idea of paragraph B?
   A. Dogs can smell anything.
   B. Dogs can be trained to identify specific scents.
   C. Rescue dogs save firefighters time.
   D. Rescue dogs can identify a person's scent.

3. In paragraph C, what are the three traits that a rescue dog needs?

   _____

   _____

   _____

4. Which sentence is the topic sentence of paragraph D?

   Sentence ____

5. Which two sentences support the idea that a dog has been trained for rescue?
   A. It refuses to eat or drink.
   B. It can recognize a specific person's smell.
   C. It isn't afraid of people.
   D. It can walk safely over debris.

   Which two paragraphs are the best evidence? ____, ____

4. The Rosetta Stone
by M. A. Hockett

A [1]Does Britain have something of great historical importance that belongs to Egypt? [2]Some people think so. [3]It is a lump of black rock! [4]But not just any black rock. [5]It is the Rosetta Stone.

B [6]The stone was carved by Egyptian priests in 196 B.C. to honor their king. [7]They wrote their message in picture symbols called hieroglyphs. [8]They also wrote the message in two other languages. [9]Then the stone was placed in a temple.

C [10]Centuries passed, and people lost track of the stone. [11]Through the years, historians found other Egyptian objects written in hieroglyphs. [12]If only they could read them! [13]They could learn much about the ancient Egyptians. [14]A message in an unknown language could be read if you compared it to similar writing in a known language. [15]There was no such "key" available to help people understand the picture symbols. [16]Not until the 18th century.

D [17]The British navy had beaten the French general, Napoleon, in Egypt. [18]The defeated Frenchmen were stuck there for several years. [19]In 1799, one of these men found a stone with writing on it in an old fort. [20]Since it was found in the town of Rosetta, they called it the "Rosetta Stone." [21]The British took it from the French and carried it back to Britain.

E [22]After it was taken to Britain, the Rosetta Stone played a big part in solving the mystery of hieroglyphs. [23]The stone's message was also written in Greek. [24]Therefore, experts who knew Greek were able to compare the Greek with the hieroglyphs. [25]They figured out what each symbol meant, and the mystery was solved! [26]Other hieroglyphic writings could then be used to study the ancient Egyptian culture.

F [27]Some people think the Rosetta Stone should be returned to Egypt. [28]After all, the stone *was* created in Egypt by Egyptians. [29]On the other hand, the British enabled the stone to teach the world about Egyptian culture and history. [30]Should the stone be returned to Egypt? [31]You decide the answer.

DIRECTIONS: Circle the letter next to the correct answer or write the answer on the lines given. When asked for evidence, write the number of the sentence or the letter of the paragraph that best supports the answer.

1. Which of the following best describes the main idea of the story?
   A. the war over the Rosetta Stone
   B. how hieroglyphs were figured out
   C. the British beat Napoleon
   D. the importance of the Rosetta Stone

2. Which paragraph tells the history of how and why the Rosetta Stone was made? _____

3. In paragraph C, people had found objects with hieroglyphic writing. What did they need in order to figure out what the writing said?
   A. historians to pick out the most important objects
   B. Egyptians willing to share their language
   C. similar writing in a known language
   D. a map of the ancient Egyptian lands

   Which two sentences are the best evidence? _____, _____

4. What is the main idea of Paragraph E?
   A. A Frenchman found the stone.
   B. It took many experts to understand the Greek writing.
   C. The Rosetta Stone helped solve a mystery.
   D. The stone had hieroglyphs and Greek.

   Which sentence is the topic sentence? _____

5. How did the experts use the Rosetta Stone?

   _____

   _____

   _____

   Which sentence is the best evidence? _____

6. In paragraph F:
   A. what sentence supports the idea that the stone should be returned to Egypt? _____
   B. what sentence supports the idea that the stone should stay in Britain? _____

DRAWING CONCLUSIONS AND MAKING INFERENCES

Drawing Conclusions

Drawing conclusions is something you do all the time. For example, Mary has to wear one of her three dresses tonight. She has a blue dress, a red dress, and an orange dress. The orange and red dresses are at the cleaners. Therefore, you can conclude she will wear the blue dress. When you read a story, you can conclude things about characters and events from the information given in the story.

Inferences and Facts

Facts are clearly stated information that can be proven. They can also suggest other ideas that are not clearly stated. An **inference** is a kind of conclusion you can make that is suggested by the facts. While you use facts as evidence for your inference, you may not be able to prove your inference is true.

See if you can tell the difference between an inference and a fact in the following story.

A   ¹The sun glistened on the new snow. ²Almost a foot had fallen since last night. ³Now the sky was clear as the bus went along. ⁴Looking out the bus window, Jorge could see it was going to be a beautiful day. ⁵"A perfect day to be sledding," thought Jorge, as his bus pulled into the school parking lot.

Fact: There was new snow.

Fact: Jorge is on a school bus.

Inference: Jorge is a student.

Inference: Jorge would rather be sledding.

The facts above are clearly stated in the story. The inferences are made by the reader using the facts as clues, or evidence.

Is the following statement a fact or an inference? _____

It is no longer snowing.

Use sentence 3 as a clue.

Examine the Evidence

When you make an inference, look at what really happens and what is suggested in the story. Often an author gives clues to suggest something he or she wants you to think. When you use evidence to make an inference, your inference could still be either true or false.

For instance, in Jorge's story, the author never says that Jorge is a student riding on the bus. The words "his bus" in sentence 5 suggest that he may be a student. However, it is also possible that Jorge is the bus driver. If the next sentence stated that he got off the bus and went to class, you would have more evidence.

Another example of making an inference is using what a character says and does to decide what kind of person he or she is. The story may not tell you directly what this person is like, so you must make a good guess based on how he or she acts. In the following story, what inference can you make about Kenny's attitude towards Mrs. P?

B   ¹I thought I might make it this time. ²I looked for Mrs. P. ³When I didn't see her in the yard, I started to walk quickly past the house. ⁴As I got to the gate, Mrs. P came around the corner of the house. ⁵"Kenny, just the person I wanted to see," she cried. ⁶"Can't stop this time, Mrs. P.; I've got to get home," I called. ⁷But she was already opening the gate for me. ⁸"It will only take a minute, Kenny. ⁹Surely, you can spare one minute for an old lady." ¹⁰She'd caught me again. ¹¹I turned and slowly walked through the gate.

1. You probably guessed that Kenny wants to avoid Mrs. P. Which three sentences are the best evidence? ____, _____, ____

2. Can you tell *why* he wants to avoid her? _____

3. Is it a fact or an inference that Mrs. P. has stopped Kenny before?

    _____

4. Which three sentences are the best evidence? ____, ____, ____

Using Your Own Knowledge

Sometimes when you make an inference, you use your own knowledge along with the information that is given or suggested in the text. Most people know that some snakes eat small animals. Can you use this information to make an inference about what happened to the gerbils?

C   [1]Amy was pet sitting Kai's pet boa constrictor. [2]When she went to check on him in the morning, the snake was missing. [3]There also seemed to be fewer gerbils in the next cage.

It is possible that the snake and the gerbils escaped together. It is more likely that the snake escaped and ate the gerbils. It is a fact that boas eat small animals, so you can use your own knowledge of boas to support this conclusion. In this case, the inference is probably true, but it could be false. There is not enough evidence given in the story for us to know what really happened to the gerbils.

Read the next paragraph.

D   [1]The plant in the corner looked like it was dying. [2]The soil was still moist, so he knew it didn't need more water. [3]And he had fertilized it just last week. [4]Only a branch nearest the window was lifted slightly. [5]The rest of the plant was drooping.

What outside information do you use to make the inference that the plant needs light?

_____

_____

INFERENCE PRACTICE ACTIVITY

Read the following story.

A ^{1}Fred slowly climbed the slippery slope. ^{2}Heavy rains had flooded the river, causing it to change its path. ^{3}Looking at the old map, he knew it would be even harder to find the spot marked with an X.

B ^{4}Suddenly the ground gave way, and Fred slid back down the hillside. ^{5}As he got up, he noticed a small opening between two large rocks. ^{6}Taking out his flashlight, he peered inside. ^{7}A sudden glimmer caught his eye. ^{8}He quickly started to pull away rocks and branches until he could fit through the opening. ^{9}Inside was a large, dark cave. ^{10}Pulling out his flashlight again, he wondered if he had only imagined that glimmer. ^{11}Then he turned and spotted a small gold coin glistening on the floor of the cave. ^{12}So the tale was true!

1. Paragraph A suggests that Fred
   A. is hiking for the day.
   B. is searching for something.
   C. is lost in the woods.
   D. is caught in a storm.

   Which sentence is the best evidence? _____

2. In paragraph B, what do you think the sudden glimmer probably was?

   _____

   Which sentence is the best evidence? _____

3. In sentence 12, the tale was probably about

   _____

5. "Bums in the Attic" from *The House on Mango Street*
by Sandra Cisneros

A [1]I want a house on a hill like the ones with the gardens where Papa works. [2]We go on Sundays, Papa's day off. [3]I used to go. [4]I don't anymore. [5]You don't like to go out with us, Papa says. [6]Getting too old? [7]Getting too stuck-up, says Nenny. [8]I don't tell them I am ashamed—all of us staring out the window like the hungry. [9]I am tired of looking at what we can't have. [10]When we win the lottery . . . Mama begins, and then I stop listening.

B [11]People who live on hills sleep so close to the stars they forget those of us who live too much on earth. [12]They don't look down at all except to be content to live on hills. [13]They have nothing to do with last week's garbage or fear of rats. [14]Night comes. [15]Nothing wakes them but the wind.

C [16]One day I'll own my own house, but I won't forget who I am or where I came from. [17]Passing bums will ask, Can I come in? [18]I'll offer them the attic, ask them to stay, because I know how it is to be without a house.

D [19]Some days after dinner, guests and I will sit in front of a fire. [20]Floorboards will squeak upstairs. [21]The attic grumble.

E [22]Rats? they'll ask.

F [23]Bums, I'll say, and I'll be happy.

DIRECTIONS: Circle the letter next to the correct answer or write the answer on the lines given. When asked for evidence, write the number of the sentence or the letter of the paragraph that best supports the answer.

1. From paragraph A, you can infer that the family probably:
   A. likes to go for Sunday drives together.
   B. can't afford a house on the hill.
   C. is content with their lives.
   D. thinks they'll win the lottery soon.

   Which three sentences are the best evidence? ____, ____, ____

2. From paragraph B, you can infer that the narrator:
   A. spends time with people who live in the hills.
   B. feels ignored by the people in the hills.
   C. fights with the people in the hills.
   D. doesn't know any people who live in the hills.

   Which two sentences support this inference? ____, ____

3. From paragraph B, you can infer that the narrator has had to put up with what three things?

   _____

   _____

   _____

   Which two sentences are the best evidence? ____, ____

4. The narrator will let bums stay in her house so:
   A. she doesn't get rats.
   B. they can sleep close to the stars.
   C. she doesn't forget where she came from.
   D. she won't be alone.

   Which two sentences are the best evidence? ____, ____

6. Secrets Revealed
by David White

A [1]Lori was angry. [2]She was also sad. [3]Her diary was missing. [4]She had brought it to school that day, just like always, and had taken it to lunch with her, to write in and to show her friends. [5]They had left their table for only a minute. [6]When she came back, the diary was missing. [7]It had been in the middle of a stack of books, right next to her purse. [8]Now, the diary was gone.

B [9]Who took it? [10]That was the main question. [11]All of her friends denied taking it. [12]She didn't really suspect them anyway.

C [13]She looked around to see who else was near. [14]She saw Ryan Bolton, Steve Larsen, and Tonya Hoying sitting at the next table. [15]They were all looking at her and snickering.

D [16]"One of them has my diary," Lori said to her friends. [17]"They don't like me. [18]I don't want them reading my private thoughts, but how do I find out which one took it?"

E [19]Maria replied, "Why don't you just go and ask them? [20]Maybe one of them will turn red and admit it."

F [21]Lori thought for a moment, then snapped her fingers. [22]"I have it!" she exclaimed and walked confidently over to the next table, where Ryan,

Steve, and Tonya were laughing to themselves.

G [23]"Hello," Lori said as she approached. [24]"I wonder if you could help me. [25]I'm missing a book, and I wonder if any of you saw me drop it anywhere."

H [26]The three suspects looked at one another and then shrugged.

I [27]"I didn't see you drop anything," Steve said.

J [28]"Me neither," Tonya said.

K [29]"Nobody wants your stupid diary anyway," Ryan said. [30]The three of them laughed and turned away from Lori.

L [31]"Ryan," Lori said, "you can give my diary back right now or I can turn you in. [32]The choice is yours."

DIRECTIONS: Circle the letter next to the correct answer or write the answer on the lines given. When asked for evidence, write the number of the sentence or the letter of the paragraph that best supports the answer.

1. From paragraph A, you can conclude that Lori's diary disappeared:
   A. on the way to school.
   B. on the way home from school.
   C. when she was away from her table during lunch.
   D. when she looked around to see who else was near.

   Which three sentences are the best evidence? _____, _____, _____

2. You can infer that Lori didn't suspect her friends because:
   A. they had already denied taking it.
   B. they hadn't had time to take it.
   C. she had asked them to watch it while she was gone.
   D. they had left with her.

   Which sentence is the best evidence? _____

3. In sentence 22, why did Lori walk "confidently" over to the next table?
   A. She thought she knew how to find out who stole her diary.
   B. She thought she'd see the diary there.
   C. Her friends had convinced her to do it.
   D. Her friends had told her who stole the diary.

4. Lori concluded that Ryan took her diary because:

   _____

   _____

   _____

   Which sentence is the best evidence? _____

5. If Lori was to check for Ryan's fingerprints, in which of these places would she most likely find them?
   A. her locker
   B. her other books
   C. her lunch tray
   D. her purse

   Which sentence is the best evidence? _____

7. Speed Skating
by Christine Broz

A [1]Speed skating is the fastest human-powered sport in the world. [2]It requires speed, strength, and the ability to make split-second decisions. [3]People who like extreme speed are attracted to this sport. [4]The goal is to fly around an oval track of ice as fast as possible. [5]Olympic speed skaters reach speeds nearing 40 m.p.h. [6]Skaters train long hours off the ice to gain the fitness needed to skate at high speeds.

B [7]Speed skating is done indoors on a short track that is 111 meters around, or on a long track, 400 meters around. [8]The races vary in length from 500 meters to 10,000 meters.

C [9]In short track competition, four or five skaters line up at the start. [10]At the sound of the starting gun, the skaters explode off the line. [11]Their skate blades dig into the ice as they sprint for the lead position. [12]Their speed increases as their arms swing powerfully across their bent-over bodies. [13]The racers then tuck one or both arms behind them to reduce the effect of the wind dragging on them.

D [14]Skating around an oval is much harder than skating in a straight line. [15]Skaters use a great deal of muscle power on the curves to overcome the centrifugal force* that can send them hurtling towards the outer edge of the track. [16]The feeling of this force is much like trying to hold onto a fast spinning merry-go-round. [17]Staying close to the inside of the curve requires great strength while maintaining speed. [18]Because of this, the skaters crouch lower as they go into a curve. [19]They put an arm out to the ice to help keep their balance. [20]The whole time, skaters risk falling.

E [21]Passing another skater is no easy task either. [22]Skaters must quickly decide when they are going to pass. [23]They bump and push each other a bit trying to gain the lead position. [24]Skaters may be disqualified for excessive pushing.

F [25]The racers streak past the finish line. [26]The winner is the skater whose skate blade crosses the finish line first. [27]Skaters say the rush of excitement from a race on ice is like nothing else. [28]It's a speed lover's dream.

*centrifugal force: a force which pulls a rotating object away from center

DIRECTIONS: Circle the letter next to the correct answer or write the answer on the lines given. When asked for evidence, write the number of the sentence or the letter of the paragraph that best supports the answer.

1. From paragraph C, you can conclude that speed skaters swing their arms to:
   A. keep their balance.
   B. look graceful.
   C. make themselves go faster.
   D. prevent others from passing.

   Which sentence is the best evidence? _____

2. From sentence 13, you can infer that racers tuck their arms behind them to:
   A. keep their balance.
   B. prevent slowing down.
   C. pass others safely.
   D. prevent bumping others.

3. In paragraph D, why is it harder to skate on a curve than on a straight path?
   A. Skaters are going faster on icy curves.
   B. Skaters are pulled to the outside by a strong force.
   C. Skaters can get dizzy on curves.
   D. Skaters don't need to crouch when skating straight.

   Which sentence is the best evidence? _____

4. Speed skaters are most likely to make split-second decisions when they:
   A. go around curves.
   B. pass the finish line.
   C. sprint off the start line.
   D. pass other skaters.

   Which sentence is the best evidence? _____

5. Based on paragraphs D and E, what two things may prevent a skater from winning a race even if she/he is the fastest?

   _____

   _____

   _____

   Which two sentences are the best evidence? _____, _____

8. The Coin
by Tom Bentley

A [1]Silvio and his best friend, Duncan, rode their bikes to the Hamburger Palace. [2]They went there together almost every weekend, one paying one week, and the other paying the next. [3]However, last week Silvio had forgotten his wallet. [4]Duncan had—with a grumble—paid again for the both of them.

B [5]Just when Silvio was about to order, he realized that he had indeed brought his wallet, but with only enough money for his own order. [6]He also had the old silver dollar that his grandfather had given to him before his recent death.

C [7]It was a beautiful old coin, heavy and smooth. [8]The sharp detail on the American Eagle was still crisp and clean. [9]Silvio loved to rub the coin, and to flip it up and snatch it out of the air. [10]He loved even more his memories of his grandfather. [11]But he couldn't make Duncan pay anything again. [12]And he was hungry—very hungry! [13]The smell of the food was overpowering. [14]He moved quickly to the counter and blurted out their orders.

D [15]"Hey, cool coin," said the counterperson as she dropped it into the register. [16]"Next order, please."

E [17]Hungry as he was, Silvio couldn't concentrate on his food. [18]He kept thinking of his grandfather's warm, still firm grip on his hand at the hospital bedside. [19]His grandfather had slipped the silver dollar in Silvio's pocket without Silvio even knowing. [20]Silvio had found it that night, the same night his grandfather died.

F [21]"Silvio, you are really somewhere else," said Duncan, jolting Silvio out of his thoughts. [22]"Let's get out of here. [23]I want to go to the mall and check out some new clothes."

G [24]Silvio didn't feel like going to the mall. [25]He rode home with a heavy heart. [26]He felt that he'd eaten the most expensive hamburger in the world— and he felt hungry for something that couldn't be found at a food counter. [27]He hoped his grandfather hadn't been watching.

DIRECTIONS: Circle the letter next to the correct answer or write the answer on the lines given. When asked for evidence, write the number of the sentence or the letter of the paragraph that best supports the answer.

1. You can infer that the coin was valuable to Silvio because:
   A. he could buy lunches for Duncan and himself.
   B. it was worth a lot of money.
   C. it was still in good condition.
   D. his grandfather gave it to him.

   Which two sentences are the best evidence? _____, _____

2. Which two paragraphs best support the inference that Silvio regretted giving away the coin?

   Paragraphs _____ and _____

3. Why do you think Silvio didn't ask Duncan to pay for the food?
   A. He was hungrier than Duncan.
   B. He was embarrassed to ask Duncan again.
   C. He knew Duncan was saving money for new clothes.
   D. His order cost more than Duncan's.

   Which two sentences are the best evidence? _____, _____

4. From the passage, you can infer that Silvio and his grandfather:
   A. disliked each other.
   B. cared about each other.
   C. spent all their time together.
   D. shared the same interests.

   Which three sentences are the best evidence? _____, _____, _____

5. What is the "somewhere else" that Duncan refers to in sentence 21?

   _____

   _____

   Which paragraph is the best evidence? _____

6. What do you think sentence 26 suggests Silvio was hungry for?
   A. another coin
   B. a chance to undo what he had done
   C. his grandfather's coin
   D. a chance to see his grandfather again

9. Clumsy Clem
by M. A. Hockett

A [1]"Nice sprawl, Clums!" [2]Garth was teasing his brother Clem, who had tripped once again over their dog, Ginger, and found himself face-to-face with a floor tile.

B [3]"You should pay attention to the *real* world," Jeb said as Clem untangled himself. [4]"And quit daydreaming about those silly potions, Dr. Wartnose!" Garth added. [5]Both brothers hooted as Clem slunked to his "lab" in the basement.

C [6]"I'll show them," he thought. [7]"When I perfect my wart remover, I'll be handsome and rich." [8]This one was going to work, he was sure! [9]But as he pried the lid, it shot off. [10]As Clem dove to pick it up, he bumped the jar. [11]"Oh, no!" Clem cried as he grabbed at it. [12]All four pints covered him from head to toe!

D [13]"Well, I guess this will be a good test," thought Clem as he got up and looked in a mirror to see if the wart would disappear.

E [14]And disappear it did! [15]Along with Clem's freckles. [16]Along with his hair. [17]In fact, along with every other part of Clem's body! [18]Clem started to panic. [19]"Help! You guys..." [20]Then he had a thought. [21]A lovely little, delicious idea. [22]He had to hurry before the "remover" wore off.

F [23]Upstairs, the boys were playing with Ginger when she started sniffing around and acting funny.

G [24]Garth grabbed a doughnut as he chuckled and said, "What's the matter, Girl? [25]You see a ghost?" [26]Suddenly, Garth plunged forward and landed headfirst on the sofa. [27]His face was completely buried in the jelly doughnut!

H [28]Jeb was coming into the living room with a plate of spaghetti, and he almost fell on the floor laughing. [29]"Woohoo! [30]Using your face to break your fall these days?"

I [31]His words were barely out when he felt himself jerked backwards. [32]Up went the plate of spaghetti. [33]And down fell the slithery strands all over his head.

J [34]"You look just like a Raggedy Ann doll!" Garth snorted as Ginger slurped spaghetti from Jeb's face. [35]Clem noticed his "remover" was wearing off and waited in the kitchen. [36]A few minutes later, he walked into the living room. [37]His brothers were still sliding in sauce.

K [38]"So *this* is what it's like in the real world!" he said. [39]They looked at him with red faces as they gave up the struggle and sat in the mess on the floor.

DIRECTIONS: Circle the letter next to the correct answer or write the answer on the lines given. When asked for evidence, write the number of the sentence or the letter of the paragraph that best supports the answer.

1. What can you conclude from paragraph A?
   A. Garth tripped his brother.
   B. Clem tripped his brother.
   C. Garth had tripped in the past.
   D. Clem had tripped in the past.

   Which sentence is the best evidence? ____

2. What can you infer about Clem's face from paragraph B?

   _____

   Which sentence is the best evidence? ____

3. What can you infer about the wart remover? Clem:
   A. has tried making it before.
   B. just got the idea to make it.
   C. wants to give it to someone else.
   D. has never told his brothers about it.

   Which sentence is the best evidence? ____

4. Clem was covered with four pints of what?

   _____

   What was the result?

   _____

5. In paragraph E, Clem's "idea" was to:
   A. change the formula for the wart remover.
   B. get his brothers to help him reappear.
   C. pay his brothers back for teasing him.
   D. get his brothers to try the wart remover.

6. Garth probably fell down because:
   A. he was pushed by Clem.
   B. he was clumsy.
   C. he tripped over Ginger.
   D. he saw a ghost.

   Which sentences give the best evidence?
   A. 19–22
   B. 20–25
   C. 26–27
   D. 28–31

7. Jeb probably looked like a Raggedy Ann doll because:
   A. his face had red spots on it.
   B. spaghetti covered his head like yarn hair.
   C. his clothes were ragged.
   D. he could bend his body like a doll.

   Which two sentences are the best evidence? ____, ____

10. From Frozen to Food, Fast
by M. A. Hockett

A [1]You take a frozen lump, set it inside the door, and push a few buttons. [2]Moments later, you hear a familiar beep and take out a piping hot burrito! [3]Have you ever wondered how a microwave oven heats food so fast?

B [4]First, think about a regular oven. [5]When the oven is on and you open the door, you feel the heat coming out. [6]That's because a heating element heats the air in this oven. [7]The hot air warms the burrito starting at the outside, so the heat needs time to move toward the inside. [8]In fact, the edges of the burrito may get brown while the center is still cold.

C [9]In a microwave oven, the air does not get hot. [10]You could say the air carries waves that help food to make its *own* heat!

D [11]When you turn on the microwave oven, the 115 volts of electricity coming from the wall outlet are boosted to 3000 volts. [12]This much electric pressure could kill you, but it is present only when the oven is operating.

E [13]Next, this pressure is changed to microwaves, which are very short radio waves. [14]The microwaves bounce off the metal walls of the oven. [15]This allows them to reach the food from many different directions.

F [16]The microwaves flip their electric fields back and forth 2,450 times per second. [17]The molecules inside the food respond by flipping back and forth along with the waves. [18]This results in a lot of bumping and shoving between molecules, and builds up friction. [19]The friction allows food to be heated evenly inside and outside.

G [20]When you reach in to check your burrito, you don't feel heat coming out of the microwave oven. [21]But could the microwaves be cooking your hand? [22]No. [23]When the door is opened, the microwaves stop. [24]It is safe to reach in and grab your hot meal!

DIRECTIONS: Circle the letter next to the correct answer or write the answer on the lines given. When asked for evidence, write the number of the sentence or the letter of the paragraph that best supports the answer.

1. To create microwaves, you can infer that a microwave oven:
   A. needs more electrical pressure than what comes from the wall.
   B. needs less electrical pressure than what comes from the wall.
   C. uses electricity exactly as it comes from the wall outlet.
   D. heats faster because it uses more electricity than a regular oven.

2. You burn your mouth on the first bite of food and freeze your teeth on the insides of the food. From the article, you can infer that the food:
   A. was not cooked in a regular oven.
   B. was not cooked in a microwave oven.
   C. was cooked on a stovetop.
   D. was cooked on a campfire.

   Which sentence is the best evidence? _____

3. From paragraph E, you can tell that microwaves probably:
   A. go through metal walls.
   B. cannot change direction.
   C. stop when they reach food.
   D. go in many directions.

   Which sentence is the best evidence? _____

4. Is each statement a fact that is given or an inference you make? Circle **G** for given, **I** for inference.
   A. A microwave is a kind of short radio wave.

          G   **I**

   B. In a microwave oven, there is friction both at the edges and in the middle of the food.

          G   **I**

5. From the article, you can tell that molecules:
   A. remain in one position.
   B. are always hot.
   C. respond to short radio waves.
   D. act like radio waves.

   Which two sentences are the best evidence? _____, _____

11. Music for the Ages
by Cheryl Block

A ¹At age 16, Ashley Berry is a young woman who knows how to get things done. ²Ashley was playing the violin for her grandmother when she realized that music was a great way to bring young and old together. ³She also thought music would be a good way to brighten the lives of other older people. ⁴She decided to start a nonprofit group called Music for the Ages. ⁵Their goal is to send students to perform in nursing homes and convalescent hospitals*.

B ⁶A family friend told Ashley how to write a request to the local Kiwanis Club for support. ⁷The Kiwanis agreed to manage the group's funds. ⁸Ashley then requested and got a $2000 grant from another local club to start the project. ⁹She went to local high schools to find students willing to perform for the seniors. ¹⁰She put together shows for the nursing homes. ¹¹Since then, Music for the Ages has been given more donations and grants. ¹²Some of this money is now going back to the schools for their music programs.

C ¹³"Every performance reminds me of my grandmother and in many ways, every performance is for her," said Ashley. ¹⁴Howard Blair, a director for Pacific Grove Convalescent Hospital, also believes that the concerts bring joy to the lives of the seniors. ¹⁵"We had three people there (at the concert) who hadn't been out of their rooms in awhile," he said. ¹⁶"It's nice when you see someone having fun when you didn't think it was possible." ¹⁷And Ashley says the students seem to enjoy themselves just as much as the seniors.

*convalescent hospital: a place for elderly patients to recover

DIRECTIONS: Circle the letter next to the correct answer or write the answer on the lines given. When asked for evidence, write the number of the sentence or the letter of the paragraph that best supports the answer.

1. From sentence 3, you can probably infer that:
   A. Ashley enjoyed playing the violin.
   B. Ashley's grandmother enjoyed her playing.
   C. all people enjoy the violin.
   D. Ashley's grandmother played the violin.

2. Which sentences support the conclusion in sentence 1 that Ashley knows how to get things done?
   A. 4, 5, 6
   B. 8, 9, 10
   C. 11, 12, 13
   D. 2, 3, 4

3. What did Ashley probably mean in sentence 13?
   A. Ashley dedicated each performance to her grandmother.
   B. Her grandmother enjoyed music.
   C. Her grandmother came to all the performances.
   D. Playing for her grandmother gave Ashley the idea for the program.

4. The name of Ashley's group probably refers to:
   A. the history of music.
   B. music for young and old.
   C. the seniors.
   D. music that stays in style.

   Which sentence is the best evidence? _____

5. From paragraph C, you can conclude that:
   A. the project is working.
   B. the project needs work.
   C. the group has failed.
   D. the group is now wealthy.

   Which two sentences are the best evidence? _____, _____

STORY ELEMENTS

Conflict

The **plot** is the series of events that take place in the story. Most plots have a main **conflict**, the problem around which the action is centered. The story beginning sets up the problem. The middle develops the conflict, and the ending solves the problem. For example, a group of kids goes camping and one of them gets lost. The middle of the story focuses on their efforts to find their lost friend and his efforts to survive in the wilderness. The main conflict is between the campers and the wilderness. A story can have more than one conflict. There could be a minor conflict between the campers about how to find their friend. The **resolution** tells how the conflict is solved. The campers contact the local rangers, who find their friend.

A conflict can be between two or more characters, or a character can have a conflict within himself when he isn't sure what to do. What kind of conflict is in the following story?

A   ¹Aaron races in the door. ²He is late for practice, but he is starved. ³He opens the refrigerator and grabs a can of soda and an apple. ⁴As he pops open the can, the dog jumps up, shaking the can and knocking it loose. ⁶Soda explodes everywhere. ⁷What a mess! ⁸He is already late. ⁹If he stays to clean up, he will be in big trouble with the coach. ¹⁰But he hates to leave a mess for his mom. ¹¹His mother arrives just as he has cleaned up. ¹²She helps him finish and then drives him to practice.

Aaron's conflict is internal. Once he decides to start cleaning up, his conflict is resolved. Read the next story.

B   ¹At the city council meeting, Shania and her friends felt ready to give up their fight for a teen center. ²The council wouldn't listen to them. ³They didn't think a teen center was important. ⁴But Shania knew it would help keep kids off the street. ⁵Then she had an idea. ⁶They could start a center in the church basement while raising the funds to build one. ⁷Would the council agree?

1. Who is the conflict between? _____

2. How will it be resolved? _____

Key Events

A story may have key events that determine what happens in the story. The **crisis** is the point in the story where the problem or conflict must be resolved. Take the example of the campers. Suppose the missing camper is injured. If he isn't found by morning, he will die from his injuries. The story has reached a crisis point. However, the camper is in an area where they had already looked, but missed seeing him. A **key event** would be the searchers' decision to take one more look in the area. Because of this decision, they find the missing camper in time.

Identifying Setting

Setting is the time and place in which a story takes place. Sometimes a story tells you the exact time and place. Other times, there are clues that suggest when and where the story takes place. What is the setting in the following story? When and where does the story take place?

C ^{1}It was so quiet. ^{2}Other than insects chirping, you couldn't hear a sound. ^{3}Moonlight filtered through the branches overhead. ^{4}He paddled along noiselessly, the oar sliding through the water like a needle through fine silk. ^{5}He still had a few hours of darkness. ^{6}Once he reached the other side, he would set out on foot.

Sentences 3 and 5 give clues that it is night. What do the words *paddled* and *oar* in sentence 4 tell you? Sentence 6 supports that he is crossing a body of water, probably a lake or river.

Time in a story can mean different things:

- The time of day.
- The length of time that passes during the story. A story may follow one brief event or a character's whole life.
- A historical time period. This is especially important in stories that take place in the past or the future.

1. During what historical period does the following story happen?

   _____

2. How much time goes by? _____

D   ¹Jeb liked it when he could drive the wagon, but most of the time he had to walk behind and tend to the animals. ²He was always covered with dust and dirt, but the worst was when it rained and the wagons bogged down in the mud. ³They had been traveling for weeks, but Pa said it could take up to six months before they reached Oregon. ⁴That was if they didn't get caught in an early snowstorm.

Weather is also part of the story setting. A storm, for instance, may affect the action in the story. Read the next paragraph.

E   ¹It hadn't rained in weeks. ²The intense heat had dried up the crops. ³We couldn't replant until the rains came. ⁴Ma's small savings was nearly gone. ⁵Pa went into town to look for work.

3. How does the weather affect the story?

_____

_____

Mood

Mood is the feeling you get from a story; the mood can be exciting or sad or funny. Setting can help define the *mood* of a story. A dark, stormy night can be a setting that creates a tense or scary mood. A party or celebration can give a happy mood.

What is the mood in the following story?

_____

F   ¹It was midnight. ²A deep moaning had awakened her. ³She sat up in bed, shivering. ⁴The moaning continued. ⁵She lit a candle and crept to the hall door. ⁶The old floor creaked; the wailing got louder. ⁷As she opened the door, a sudden draft blew out her light. ⁸Something moved in the hallway.

Analyzing Characters

Characters' words and actions keep a story moving. These words and actions can also tell you about a character's traits, or what kind of person he or she is. **Character traits** describe a person's qualities. A character may be kind or mean, silly or serious, brave or shy. You learn what a character is like as you watch what he or she does and says. Read the next story:

G   ¹"Has anyone seen my new pen?" asked Mrs. Chan. ²"I laid it right here on my desk." ³As I looked at her desk I had no idea where "right here" might be. ⁴There wasn't an empty space anywhere. ⁵Some piles were a foot deep. ⁶Mrs. Chan never got rid of anything. ⁷Who knew what lurked in those desk drawers? ⁸The last time I helped her look for something, I found last month's birthday cake still sitting on a plate.

1. What trait would you use to describe Mrs. Chan?

     A. tidy

     B. messy

     C. forgetful

     D. strict

2. Which four sentences are the best evidence? _____, _____, _____, _____

Point of View

The **narrator** is the person who is telling the story. The narrator may tell the story as a character himself or may describe the actions of all the characters in the story. **Point of view** refers to how the events of the story are seen. A story can be told from the viewpoint of only one character or through the eyes of several different characters.

H   ¹I always looked up to Scott. ²He was much older than I was, but people said that we looked a lot alike. ³He treated me like a little kid, even when I grew up. ⁴But there came a time when I had to look out for him. ⁵It happened the year that our dad died.

1. From whose viewpoint is the story told? _____

2. Who is the narrator? _____

12. He's Got Mail
by M. A. Hockett

You've got mail!

A [1]Ryder Hall couldn't keep still. [2]His e-mail program had just said, "You've got mail." [3]Would it be from the unknown girl who called herself Runner, he wondered? [4]He'd have to wait and see. [5]That nosy Emily Kudras had just poked her head around the corner of the computer lab. [6]Rats! [7]If only he had remembered to turn his sound off. [8]At least he was fast enough to click on the history site that was waiting in the background. [9]If she knew he was e-mailing in class, she'd probably tell Ms. Steinmetz. [10]Emily was such a pain.

B [11]Not like Runner. [12]She was the coolest girl Ryder knew. [13]She liked swimming and running and listening to music. [14]And she had trouble making friends—just like he did. [15]She said people didn't understand her. [16]She wanted to talk to them, but she didn't know how. [17]When she asked questions, they would say she was a snoop. [18]Then she would end up crying and going off by herself.

C [19]"What are you doing now, Ryder?" a voice suddenly jolted him.

D [20]It was Emily again. [21]What a pain. [22]"None of your business, *Snoop,*" he quickly shot back. [23]He didn't see her tears as she left the room.

E [24]"Thank goodness," he thought as he opened his email. [25]Now he could see what Runner had to say.

F [26]*Trackman,*

[27]*At least I can talk to you. [28]There's this boy that I like in my lab. [29]But whenever I try to talk to him, he ignores me or calls me an awful name. [30]I'm going to try once more. [31]If he's mean again, I'm going to need your advice. [32]Wish me luck! [33]Gotta go— Ms. Steinmetz is coming.*

[34]*Runner*

G [35]Ryder sat still in his chair as the truth dawned on him. [36]Emily, who ran to school listening to CDs and spent hours in the pool—Emily, who seemed to be so nosy, was just trying to get to know him.

H [37]He knew what his advice would be to Runner. [38]He hurried to catch up with her and tell her to give Trackman a second chance.

DIRECTIONS: Circle the letter next to the correct answer or write the answer on the lines given. When asked for evidence, write the number of the sentence or the letter of the paragraph that best supports the answer.

1. Which of the following best describes Ryder's problem in the beginning of the story?
   A. He may get kicked out of the lab for cheating.
   B. Emily keeps him from reading his email.
   C. Emily tells Ms. Steinmetz that he's not doing his work.
   D. He needs to write a new email.

2. The main conflict in the story is between:
   A. Trackman and Runner.
   B. Runner and Emily.
   C. Ryder and Runner.
   D. Ryder and Emily.

3. Ryder's problem takes an unexpected twist. How does his problem change? He realizes he:
   A. hurt the girl he wanted to get to know.
   B. accidentally deleted the e-mail he was trying to save.
   C. succeeded in getting rid of Emily for good.
   D. must tell Runner he is interested in only Emily.

   Which paragraph is the best evidence? _____

4. How do you think Ryder intends to resolve his problem?

   _____

   _____

   Which sentence is the best evidence? _____

5. Where does the story take place?

   _____

   Which two sentences are the best evidence? _____, _____

6. Who is Ms. Steinmetz?
   A. Emily's mom
   B. the teacher
   C. the principal
   D. Emily's coach

7. Emily shows which of the following traits in the story? She:
   A. is carefree.
   B. likes to argue.
   C. doesn't give up.
   D. is gossipy.

   Which paragraph is the best evidence? _____

13. Boat People
by Cheryl Block

A [1]Phan Hui's voice was barely a whisper as he described to rescuers his family's journey to freedom. [2]Several families from his small village in Vietnam had paid the fishermen for passage to Thailand. [3]They were packed like animals into the cargo hold* of the small boat. [4]The crew hid them below deck most of the time. [5]The rough seas made people constantly sick. [6]The stale air in the hold and the awful stench added to their discomfort. [7]There was not enough food or water; the crew kept most of it for themselves.

B [8]Off the coast of Thailand, they were struck by a hurricane. [9]Huge waves beat down on the tiny boat. [10]The waves crashed over the sides of the boat, sweeping everything off the deck. [11]Then water poured into the hold. [12]Phan Hui and his little sister struggled up the ladder to the deck. [13]Their parents were still below. [14]The crew had already taken the lifeboats and abandoned their human cargo, leaving them to save themselves.

C [15]The boat had begun to break apart under the constant beating from the waves. [16]Phan's voice cracked when he described how the people in the hold, including his parents, drowned without ever making it to the deck. [17]Phan had grabbed his sister as they were swept overboard. [18]He helped her climb onto some passing debris, then clung tightly to its edges. [19]He pushed them away as the boat came apart.

D [20]When the storm finally broke, the boat had been destroyed. [21]They drifted for days, clinging to its remains. [22]There was no relief from the cold water, but the constant drizzle provided enough water to sustain them. [23]Only a few other people had survived, but gradually, one by one, they all succumbed to the cold water. [24]The circling sharks removed all trace of them, yet strangely had spared Phan and his sister. [25]Phan never let go of her.

E [26]On the third day, Phan spotted a distant ship. [27]He gathered his remaining strength and pushed them towards the ship. [28]Eventually, they were seen and picked up by the crew. [29]Now he sat huddled on the deck, wrapped in blankets, while he shared his remarkable tale.

*hold: lower interior of a ship where cargo is stored

DIRECTIONS: Circle the letter next to the correct answer or write the answer on the lines given. When asked for evidence, write the number of the sentence or the letter of the paragraph that best supports the answer.

1. How does the crew treat the families? The crew:
   A. was afraid of them.
   B. cared about their well-being.
   C. wanted them gone.
   D. treated them like cargo.

   Which two sentences are the best evidence? ____, ____

2. The main conflict in the story is between:
   A. the fishermen and the families.
   B. the survivors and nature.
   C. Phan and the crew.
   D. the boat and the hurricane.

   Explain your answer.

   _____

   _____

   _____

3. Phan's treatment of his sister shows that he was:
   A. careless.
   B. frightened.
   C. responsible.
   D. selfish.

   Which two sentences in paragraph C are the best evidence? ____,

   ____

4. The story reaches a crisis point when:
   A. there is not enough food or water.
   B. the boat is destroyed.
   C. the crew leaves the boat.
   D. Phan and his sister swim for the rescue ship.

5. From where is Phan telling his story?
   A. in the ocean
   B. on a small fishing boat
   C. on the rescue ship
   D. on an island

   Which two sentences are the best evidence? ____, ____

14. Cross Country
by Christine Broz

A [1]A year ago I was miserable. [2]My parents had just told me that we were moving from Southern California to New England. [3]My mother had been promoted to vice president of her company and that meant a move to their office near Boston. [4]My father worked as a technical writer and could work from anywhere.

B [5]It didn't seem fair! [6]I was going to start my senior year in high school, and I could not understand why my parents wouldn't wait to move until after I graduated. [7]I had a girlfriend and lots of friends. [8]My sister had just graduated, and I wanted to stay in California with her. [9]My parents said, "No way." [10]I wanted to run away.

C [11]When moving day came, I knew my worst nightmare had really come true. [12]For the next two weeks before summer ended, I moped around our new house. [13]I felt very lonely for my old friends and everything that was familiar to me.

D [14]The dreaded first day of school came, and I discovered that the kids at my high school were very friendly. [15]As a new kid, I got lots of attention. [16]I talked and dressed differently from them. [17]To my surprise, they thought being different was cool.

E [18]I finally realized I could be myself in this new place. [19]It was a relief not to have to work to impress anyone. [20]The kids were not status conscious like at my old school, where everyone was overly concerned with who had the newest gadget or the most expensive clothes.

F [21]My new school also had interesting kinds of classes that I had never had before, like woodworking and drama. [22]I began to think the move was not so bad after all.

G [23]In another three months from now, I will be going away to college. [24]I am no longer nervous about going to a new place. [25]I've learned that change can be a good thing.

DIRECTIONS: Circle the letter next to the correct answer or write the answer on the lines given. When asked for evidence, write the number of the sentence or the letter of the paragraph that best supports the answer.

1. Summarize the story plot.

   _____

   _____

   _____

   _____

2. Where is the end of the story set?
   A. California
   B. New York
   C. New England
   D. Washington

   Which sentence is the best evidence? _____

3. Who is the main character?
   A. a college senior
   B. a high school senior
   C. a runaway teen
   D. a writer for a high tech company

   Which sentence is the best evidence? _____

4. The main conflict is between

   _____

   and _____

   Which paragraph is the best evidence? _____

5. How does the narrator feel about the people in the new place?
   A. He feels they are not friendly.
   B. He feels they are just like him.
   C. He feels old compared to them.
   D. He feels accepted by them.

   Which paragraph is the best evidence? _____

6. The narrator was unhappy at the beginning of the story but felt better at the end of the story. Which paragraph shows when the narrator's feelings start to change?

   Paragraph _____

7. Over what period of time does the story take place?
   A. two weeks
   B. three months
   C. twelve months
   D. two years

   Which sentence is the best evidence? _____

15. A Run Through the Park
by David White

A [1]Her footsteps echoed in the eerie silence, the only sound she could hear on this chilly, foggy night. [2]The tall streetlights shone dimly through the fog that settled low on the city. [3]She couldn't see much, except for the occasional ghostly image of someone passing by. [4]Everyone who had any sense was at home and warm on this dreary evening. [5]Not Fernanda. [6]She was in training for a marathon, and this was her night to run long in the park.

B [7]People said ghosts populated the park on foggy nights, but she didn't believe them. [8]Her friends said they would be happy to run with her the following morning. [9]She was on a schedule. [10]She *had* to run tonight.

C [11]She was humming to herself as she settled into a good pace. [12]It was a few seconds before she noticed the harmony. [13]She stopped. [14]Silence. [15]She started running again and then began to hum again.

D [16]The harmony returned, louder this time. [17]She slowed down, looking all around her, first up above at the billowing fog and then in a slow circle all the way around. [18]It was then she realized that she was lost. [19]She was sure she had been running her usual route, yet she had no idea where to go from here.

E [20]Sensing that someone was near, she looked quickly to her right but saw nothing. [21]A quicker glance to her left revealed a shadowy figure. [22]Oddly, it seemed to be wearing a T-shirt, hat, shorts, and shoes. [23]Was this a ghost runner? [24]It started running, looking back as if it wanted her to follow. [25]She wondered if she should. [26]It seemed to know where it was going. [27]Should she take a chance that this figure would lead her out of the park? [28]When the runner was almost out of sight, Fernanda made her decision and took off after it.

F [29]The more she tried to catch up to it, the faster the ghostly figure ran. [30]She called to it but got no answer. [31]She started humming again but heard no harmony. [32]Curious more than afraid, she sprinted, hoping to catch up.

G [33]Before she knew it, she was at the edge of the park, at the end of her route. [34]She stopped running and clicked her watch off. [35]Her lungs burned. [36]There was no sign of the ghostly runner. [37]She looked down at her watch, at the very fast time recorded there, and smiled.

H [38]Her friends would never believe what a good *time* she had.

DIRECTIONS: Circle the letter next to the correct answer or write the answer on the lines given. When asked for evidence, write the number of the sentence or the letter of the paragraph that best supports the answer.

1. List three words from paragraph A that tell you what kind of night it is outside.

   _____

   _____

   _____

2. Which of these things does NOT happen in the story?
   A. Fernanda runs through the park at night.
   B. Fernanda runs with her friends through the park.
   C. Fernanda gets lost while running in the park.
   D. Fernanda hums while she runs through the park.

3. Number the following events in the story in the order in which they actually occurred.

   Fernanda:
   ___ realizes she is lost.
   ___ hears stories about ghosts in the park.
   ___ starts sprinting.
   ___ sees a ghostly figure.

4. From her actions in the story, you could describe Fernanda as:
   A. frightened.
   B. friendly.
   C. fearless.
   D. frustrated.

   Which two paragraphs are the best evidence? ____, ____

5. Describe Fernanda's conflict in paragraph E.

   _____

   _____

   _____

   How does she resolve the conflict?

   _____

   _____

LITERARY DEVICES

Flashback

A **flashback** is a jump from the present to the past. It describes events that happened at an earlier time. For example, a story may begin with an event in present time. Then the author may have the main character "flash back" to an earlier time. Unlike a memory, in a flashback, the character finds himself reliving a past event, as if it was happening again. Flashbacks can give us information about what is happening in the present or why a character is behaving a certain way. Which part of the following story is a flashback?

A   [1]The pain is really bad. [2]If only he could turn back the clock. [3]He could hear dad warning him about hiking after a storm. [4]"You know there are always slides after a heavy rain. [5]Wait a day or two until the ground settles." [6]Now, here he lies at the bottom of the ravine.

Sentences 3, 4, and 5 go back in time to give us information that help to explain what is happening now. Sentences 1, 2, and 6 are in the present.

Foreshadowing

When an author gives you a hint about what is going to happen later it is called **foreshadowing**. In the next story, decide how the author gives you clues that a storm may be coming.

B   [1]As I stepped outside, the air was hot and unusually still. [2]It was very quiet. [3]Not even a bird was singing. [4]The animals in the barn were restless. [5]I shook off a feeling of unease and started my chores.

The words "unusually still" in sentence 1 are the first clue that the weather is different. Sentences 2 and 3 suggest a change in the animals. The narrator's uneasiness is also a clue that something is going to happen.

1. Is the following flashback or foreshadowing? _____

C   [1]Joan looked at the crumpled wreckage. [2]Gia's smiling face floated before her, waving as she climbed in the car. [3]Now Gia lay in the ambulance, fighting for her life.

Symbolism

In **symbolism**, an author uses an object to stand for, or symbolize, an abstract idea or concept. For example, the Statue of Liberty is a symbol of freedom. A rock might be used as a symbol of strength.

D   [1] I had been so beaten down for so long. [2] First losing my job, and then my family. [3] Yet, I was starting to feel hopeful. [4] Things were going to change. [5] Maybe today's job interview would turn out okay. [6] Just then I saw the bud of a new crocus poking up through the blanket of old snow.

1. What object is used as a symbol? _____

2. Explain what you think it symbolizes.

  _____

  _____

16. *The Face on the Milk Carton* (Excerpt)
by Caroline B. Cooney

A [1]The little girl on the back of the carton stared back at her.

B [2]It wasn't much of a picture. [3]After all, how good could a picture be when it was printed on a milk carton?

C [4]"You ready for that algebra test?" Jason asked Adair.

D [5]"I was ready till I ate cafeteria food. [6]Do you think he'll let me out of the test if I have food poisoning?"

E [7]The girl on the carton was an ordinary little girl. [8]Hair in tight pigtails, one against each thin cheek. [9]A dress with a narrow white collar. [10]The dress was white with tiny dark polka dots.

F [11]Something evil and thick settled on Janie, blocking her throat, dimming her eyes. [12]"Sarah-Charlotte," she said. [13]She could hear herself shouting Sarah-Charlotte's name, yet her lips were not moving; she was making no sound at all.

G [14]She reached toward Sarah-Charlotte's sleeve, but her hand didn't obey. [15]It lay motionless on top of the carton. [16]It looked like somebody else's hand; she could not imagine herself wearing that shade of nail polish, or that silly ring.

H [17]"You drank my milk," accused Sarah-Charlotte.

I [18]"It's me on there," Janie whispered. [19]Her head hurt. [20]Was the milk allergy already settling in? [21]Or was she going insane? [22]Could you go insane this fast? [23]Surely it took years to lose your mind.

J [24]She imagined people losing their minds the way you might lose a penny, or your car keys—accidentally dropping your mind in the cafeteria.

K [25]"On where?" said Peter.

L [26]"The girl on the back of the carton," whispered Janie. [27]How flat her voice sounded. [28]As if she had ironed it. [29]"It's me."

M [30]She remembered that dress… [31]how the collar itched… [32]remembered the fabric; the wind blew through it… [33]remembered how those braids swung like red silk against her cheeks.

N [34]"I know you're sick of school," said Sarah-Charlotte, "but claiming to be kidnapped is going a little too far, Janie."

DIRECTIONS: Circle the letter next to the correct answer or write the answer on the lines given. When asked for evidence, write the number of the sentence or the letter of the paragraph that best supports the answer.

1. Which of the following best describes the story's setting?
   A. school cafeteria
   B. study hall
   C. playground
   D. restaurant

2. Which paragraphs give evidence that Janie has a conflict within herself?
   A. C, D
   B. H, K
   C. G, I
   D. M, N

3. In which paragraph does Janie relive a childhood scene?_____

   This is an example of
   A. mood.
   B. foreshadowing.
   C. setting.
   D. flashback.

4. The story is told from whose point of view?
   A. the teacher's
   B. Janie's
   C. Sarah-Charlotte's
   D. Peter's

   Which paragraph best supports your answer? Circle one letter.

   D   F   K   N

5. When Janie says her picture is on the carton, Sarah-Charlotte's reaction is one of:
   A. disbelief.
   B. sickness.
   C. agreement.
   D. fear.

   Which sentence is the best evidence? ____

6. The author uses physical changes in Janie to show her:
   A. growing confusion.
   B. increasing illness.
   C. lessening insanity.
   D. pleased excitement.

   Give two examples of physical changes.

   _____

   _____

17. The Pink Umbrella
by Cheryl Block

A [1]Yolanda had seen the black sedan on her street before, cruising slowly past the bus stop where the children waited each morning. [2]It seemed a little strange that the car always slowed in front of the bus stop. [3]She had never seen anyone get out of the car. [4]But she was usually in such a hurry to get to work that she probably didn't notice the car stopping.

B [5]This morning was gray and drizzly. [6]It was still early, so only one little girl with a bright pink umbrella stood waiting for the bus. [7]As Yolanda got into her car, the black sedan came around the corner. [8]This time it stopped at the bus stop.

C [9]"Probably dropping off a child," she thought as the car door opened. [10]She started her car engine. [11]But no child got out. [12]The little girl at the bus stop walked up to the sedan.

D [13]As Yolanda started to back out of the driveway, she saw an arm reach out from the black car. [14]She noticed the little girl step back. [15]Yolanda turned her head to check for oncoming cars. [16]Looking back at the bus stop, she saw that the little girl was gone.

E [17]Then she saw the pink umbrella lying on the sidewalk. [18]"Something's not right," Yolanda thought. [19]She wondered if she should call someone. [20]Grabbing her cell phone, she hit 911. [21]When the operator answered, Yolanda yelled that she thought a child was being abducted* at the corner of Oak and Hill Streets. [22]She tried reading the license plate numbers through the rainy windshield.

F [23]The black sedan started to pull away from the curb. [24]"Should I do something?" Yolanda wondered. [25]Dropping the phone, she hit the gas and slammed into the rear of the sedan. [26]The startled driver hit the brakes. [27]Yolanda pulled around in front of the sedan, blocking its way. [28]She heard sirens coming. [29]The passenger door of the sedan opened, and the little girl fell onto the sidewalk. [30]The door slammed shut. [31]Suddenly, the sedan backed up and sped away. [32]Yolanda didn't follow. [33]Seeing the flashing lights approach, she knew the kidnapper wouldn't get far. [34]She turned off the engine and ran to the little girl sitting on the sidewalk.

*abducted: taken by force

DIRECTIONS: Circle the letter next to the correct answer or write the answer on the lines given. When asked for evidence, write the number of the sentence or the letter of the paragraph that best supports the answer.

1. Yolanda could be described as:
   A. easily distracted.
   B. uncaring.
   C. very organized.
   D. quick thinking.

   Which two paragraphs are the best evidence? ____, ____

2. What clue in paragraph A foreshadows the attempted kidnapping?

   _____

   _____

   Which two sentences are the best evidence? ____, ____

3. How does the weather add to the mood of the story? The gray day makes the mood:
   A. rainy.
   B. gloomy.
   C. exciting.
   D. boring.

4. How does the author use the pink umbrella as a symbol?

   _____

   _____

   _____

   _____

5. What is Yolanda's conflict in the story? She is trying to:
   A. get to work on time.
   B. decide if something is wrong.
   C. decide if she should act.
   D. read the license plate.

   Which two sentences are the best evidence? ____, ____

6. Which event helps to resolve the story?
   A. The black car starts to pull away.
   B. Yolanda hears sirens coming.
   C. The little girl falls to the sidewalk.
   D. Yolanda slams into the car.

18. Out in the Cold
by M. A. Hockett

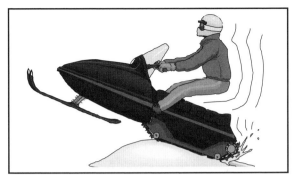

A [1]Crisp air stung at her cheeks as rocks and trees flew by. [2]The SnoKat roared beneath her as it bobbed over hills. [3]At the last snow-covered knoll, Ruthie felt suspended in midair just before the machine's weight, and then her own, sank back into the groove of the trail. [4]The tread grabbed the snowpack and surged forward.

B [5]Ruthie was too young to drive a car, so she was glad to be allowed to use the snowmobile. [6]Pa had argued against it. [7]"A young girl on a machine like that? [8]She can't handle it…" [9]But it belonged to her older brother, and he had come to her rescue. [10]"Come on," he said, "Ruthie needs some fun, Pa. [11]Besides, she's old enough to handle the Kat."

C [12]Now, Ruthie closed her eyes and said a silent thanks to her brother.

D [13]She didn't see the possum until she was almost on it. [14]She swerved. [15]"—Whoa, where did the trail go?" Ruthie said out loud. [16]"Ouch!" [17]A branch had slapped at her face.

E [18]The Kat bogged down and came to a dead stop. [19]She tried giving it more gas. [20]Nothing. [21]She tried rocking back and forth, but that didn't help. [22]She tried pulling up the back to swing it around, but it was stuck. [23]Whenever she gave it gas, the engine roared but the machine sat stubbornly still.

F [24]Exhausted, Ruthie finally collapsed across the leather seat of the Kat. [25]She could just hear Pa talking about her. [26]"I knew it!" he'd say. [27]"Stuck in the middle of nowhere, and can't get herself out of a mess." [28]Maybe he was right. [29]She sure felt helpless now. [30]It would be getting dark soon, and she was far from the house. [31]"I must have rocks in my head to think I could handle this machine," she thought.

G [32]"Rocks. [33]Hmm…" [34]She got out. [35]She felt under the buried skis until she came to a hard object. [36]The ski had gone up slightly onto a rock, so the tread could no longer dig into the snow.

H [37]Excited now, she gathered branches and shoved them under the tread. [38]Then she got back on the machine and gave it a little gas until it started moving. [39]She gave it more and more and didn't dare stop until she was safely back on the trail.

I [40]"A little late, aren't you?" asked Pa when she got home.

J [41]"Yeah, I had a little trouble with the Kat, but nothing I couldn't take care of myself," she said as she turned away with a secret smile.

DIRECTIONS: Circle the letter next to the correct answer or write the answer on the lines given. When asked for evidence, write the number of the sentence or the letter of the paragraph that best supports the answer.

1. The *main* story conflict is between:
    A. Ruthie and her brother.
    B. Pa and the SnoKat.
    C. Ruthie and the SnoKat.
    D. Pa and Ruthie's brother.

    Which paragraph is the best evidence? _____

2. Which of the following shows how Ruthie's father felt about her taking the SnoKat?
    A. doubting
    B. enthusiastic
    C. accepting
    D. resentful

    Which three sentences are the best evidence? _____, _____, _____

3. The story suggests Ruthie is capable. Which paragraph supports this inference? _____

4. Which choice below best describes the setting of the story?
    A. crisp mountain day
    B. snow-covered hills
    C. cold summer day
    D. flat snowy meadow

    Which paragraph is the best evidence? _____

5. Which paragraph contains a flashback, or description of something that happened earlier?

    Paragraph _____

6. Something foreshadowed Ruthie's discovery of the rock. What was it that made her think to check for a rock under the SnoKat? She:
    A. saw a rock beside the SnoKat.
    B. remembered Pa's warnings.
    C. had felt the SnoKat hit something hard before the knoll.
    D. had been thinking about rocks in a different way.

    Which sentence is the best evidence? _____

IDENTIFYING THEME

Finding the Theme

The theme of a story is the meaning behind the events. A theme presents large issues of human nature such as friendship or courage. Friendship is an important theme in many stories, such as *The Adventures of Tom Sawyer.*

The theme is woven throughout the story. It may be stated directly, or it may be suggested by the characters and events. Authors often show the theme through the characters' actions and words. Remember the fable about the tortoise and the hare? The hare and the tortoise have a race. The hare is a much faster runner, but he plays around during the race. He even stops to take a nap. The tortoise keeps on going, slowly but surely, and wins the race while the hare is napping. What might be a good theme for this fable? "Slow and steady wins the race" or "Never give up" are two possibilities.

When you look for the theme in the story, think about the plot. What problem, or conflict, is presented in the story? How do the characters feel about the problem? What do they do to solve it? Think about the theme for the fable above. What truth is shown by the events in the story? What did the tortoise do that supported the theme?

Now read the following story.

¹Beni loves to watch baseball, but he has used up all his money on this game. ²Now the game is over.

³As he gets up to leave, he finds a wallet on the bench. ⁴It has $10 in it. ⁵That's enough to get him a ticket to another game! ⁶He could keep the money and leave the wallet. ⁷But that wallet and money belong to someone else. ⁸He would feel guilty. ⁹He looks inside the wallet for a name.

^{10}"Oliver! ^{11}Oliver Randall!" he shouts. ^{12}Oliver Randall is down by the exit, but he comes back.

^{13}Oliver is surprised to see his wallet. ^{14}"I didn't even know I lost it!" he says. ^{15}"I'm so happy to get it back." ^{16}He pulls something from his pocket. ^{17}He says, "I want you to have my extra tickets to the rest of the games."

1. Which of the following is the best theme for this story?

   A. Ballgames are only for the rich.

   B. Sporting events are exciting.

   C. Cheating can get you more tickets.

   D. Honesty is more rewarding than cheating.

What problem is presented in the story? Beni doesn't have enough money to go to more games. Then he finds a wallet with money.

What is Beni's conflict in the story? He has to decide what to do with the money. If he gives the money back, he can't go to another game. If he keeps it, he will feel guilty.

What does Beni do to solve this? He decides to find the owner and give it back.

Which of the choices above are supported by the events in the story? There is no real evidence given in the story to support choice A. Choice B is probably true, but it is not the central idea of the story. Choice C is suggested by sentences 5 and 6, but it is not proven by the rest of the story. Choice D is the best answer. It is supported by Beni's actions in the story and the final result of the story in sentence 17.

19. *Sarny* (Excerpt)
by Gary Paulsen

A [1]The reading didn't spread so fast at first.

B [2]Took on to be slow, like watching spilled molasses smearing across a table. [3]Nightjohn he was gone but I got to where the letters meant more all the time and pretty soon I was working words with two and even three parts in them, writing whole sentences helping others and before too long some were doing the same.

C [4]Women at first, because they had the time and some kind of toughness so they could learn at night even after working in the day. [5]Men a little slower. [6]They worked until they dropped, busted and sore and didn't have much left for learning, but they did just the same, only slower.

D [7]Came a day maybe a year after Nightjohn he was gone, came a day when it changed. [8]One day it seemed people were having trouble with the words and some would stammer at them and make them slow and with thick sounds and the next day it was different. [9]Seemed everybody was reading and then it spread, oh my yes, it spread like a fire in dry grass.

E [10]One would help two and two would help four and nearly everybody came to know reading and writing and then it went to other plantations and they tried to stop it.

F [11]The men with whips and dogs they tried to stop it because they knew, they knew what it meant. [12]Meant we were learning, coming to know how it was other places other times.

G [13]Places and times where there weren't slaves, where one didn't own another, couldn't own another by law. [14]And then, some who read and some who didn't, but just listened to the ones who read, some started to run. [15]Run north.

DIRECTIONS: Circle the letter next to the correct answer or write the answer on the lines given. When asked for evidence, write the number of the sentence or the letter of the paragraph that best supports the answer.

1. Which of the following best describes the theme of the story?
   A. Running north solves many problems.
   B. Learning is worthwhile because it brings knowledge.
   C. Some people read faster than others.
   D. Owning slaves is wrong unless you let them read.

2. The men probably took longer learning to read because:
   A. They didn't really want to learn.
   B. The women were not good teachers for them.
   C. They were slower at everything they did.
   D. Their hard work left them tired.

   Which sentence is the best evidence? _____

3. In paragraph E, reading had started to spread. Which of the following gives the best reason why this happened?
   A. Some people tried to stop it.
   B. Other plantations heard about it.
   C. Each reader taught more than one person.
   D. Each student wanted to learn to write well.

4. What is the main idea of paragraph G?
   A. Slaves ran north because of what they or others read.
   B. In some places, no one could own another person.
   C. No one could ever own slaves.
   D. Slaves slowly moved north.

5. For the slave owners, what was the danger in letting slaves learn to read? The slaves would:
   A. not have enough time to do their work.
   B. make their masters look stupid and slow.
   C. start reading about all the family's secrets.
   D. read about places where they could be free.

   Which two sentences are the best evidence? _____, _____

20. Dolphin Dreams
by Christine Broz

A [1]Jane worked after school and Saturdays in the local coffee shop. [2]She spent most of her time either working or studying. [3]Sometimes she wished she could be with her friends or playing softball. [4]She had been saving her money all year for something special, her dream. [5]She dreamed of studying dolphins.

B [6]Often while she was pouring coffee, her customers would comment about her silver ring with dolphins going round it. [7]She told everyone of her dream. [8]She had been accepted into a summer program in Florida as an intern. [9]This was finally her chance to swim with dolphins. [10]However, she had to come up with the money herself to pay for the program and the airfare from Colorado to Florida.

C [11]Now, Jane had just two weeks to finish earning the money. [12]She still needed three hundred dollars. [13]She thought she could make it! [14]Then on Friday afternoon, a large party of diners left without paying their $75 bill. [15]Jane's boss insisted that it was her fault and deducted the bill from her pay. [16]Jane left work that day with tear-stained cheeks. [17]She felt like quitting, but knew it would not help her get any closer to her dream.

D [18]Later the following week, Jane found an envelope beneath an empty coffee cup at the counter. [19]A quiet old man with thick eyeglasses had been sitting there earlier. [20]He was a regular customer who stopped in nearly every afternoon for a cup of coffee and a piece of pie. [21]Inside the envelope were two pieces of paper. [22]The first one said, "Follow your dreams. [23]As a child I dreamed of flying. [24]But instead, I ended up working thirty-five years underground in the coal mines of West Virginia. [25]Now my eyesight is so poor that I can barely see the planes take off at the airfield, much less fly one. [26]You have done a great job staying focused on your dream."

E [27]Jane unfolded the second piece of paper. [28]It was a check with her name on it. [29]Her smile spread from ear to ear as she hugged the check to her chest.

DIRECTIONS: Circle the letter next to the correct answer or write the answer on the lines given. When asked for evidence, write the number of the sentence or the letter of the paragraph that best supports the answer.

1. Which of the following best describes the theme for this story?
   A. Some dreams are disappointing.
   B. If you trust people, they will take advantage of you.
   C. Some people are luckier than others.
   D. Don't give up on your dreams.

2. What is the main problem in the story?
   A. Jane doesn't get along with her boss.
   B. Jane needs enough money for the program.
   C. The old man can no longer see well.
   D. Jane wishes she could be with her friends.

   Which two sentences are the best evidence? ____, ____

3. When does the story reach a crisis?
   A. Jane has two weeks to finish earning the money.
   B. Jane's boss takes $75 from her pay.
   C. Jane decides to quit her job.
   D. Jane still needs three hundred dollars.

4. How is the problem resolved?

   _____

   _____

   Which sentence is the best evidence? ____

5. What do Jane and the old man have in common?
   A. They like coffee.
   B. Their hobby is flying.
   C. They each have a dream.
   D. Their dreams became real.

   Which two sentences are the best evidence? ____, ____

6. Why does the old man tell Jane to follow her dreams?
   A. He regretted not following his own dream.
   B. He feels too old to dream.
   C. He likes her dream better than his.
   D. He wants to help dolphins.

   Which three sentences give the best evidence? ___, ___, ___

21. The Trick
by Tom Bentley

A ¹Maria scowled and rubbed her right knee. ²She was sitting on the rough pavement of the warehouse parking lot. ³Her skateboard was lying on its back several feet away. ⁴She had been trying for the last half-hour to "grind," to ride the axle of her board on the curb's edge for a distance. ⁵However, every time the board caught the curbside, she'd been flung to the ground.

B ⁶Worse yet, her friend—and skateboarding rival—Randall had successfully done the same trick three rides in a row.

C ⁷"Hey, Maria, your moves are crude. ⁸It might be time to go back to training wheels before that knee turns to pasta," Randall said with a laugh.

D ⁹He walked over to Maria and said, "It's not like you're a bad skater or anything, but some tricks are better left to the men." ¹⁰He grinned and offered her a hand up.

E ¹¹"Yeah, yeah, so you're better at skateboarding," she said with a frown. ¹²She took his hand and stood up. ¹³"And the only MEN I see around here are those warehouse guys over there," she said with a smirk.

F ¹⁴She flipped her skateboard over with her foot and kicked down on its tail to flip it up into her hand.

¹⁵"Do you remember when a certain guy didn't get how to do a geometry problem, and a certain girl helped him with it? ¹⁶That's how people learn things, not by people making fun of their ignorance."

G ¹⁷Randall groaned and started to say something back. ¹⁸Then he stopped and wiped his forehead. ¹⁹"OK," he said. ²⁰"The deal is that you're putting too much weight on your front foot too soon. ²¹Hang back a little on the front wheels before you shift your weight."

H ²²Maria looked at him, smiled, and got on her board. ²³She approached the curb at a good speed, kicked the board up, and rode the board on the curb's edge for a good distance.

I ²⁴She rode back up to Randall. ²⁵"Not bad, not bad," he said.

J ²⁶"Just think what I could have done if I weren't a girl!" Maria retorted. ²⁷She looked at him, and they both burst out laughing.

DIRECTIONS: Circle the letter next to the correct answer or write the answer on the lines given. When asked for evidence, write the number of the sentence or the letter of the paragraph that best supports the answer.

1. Which of the following is the best theme for this story?
   A. Don't judge a book by its cover.
   B. People can learn if they're willing to help one another.
   C. Skateboarding is for boys only.
   D. Practice makes perfect.

2. Which of the following is the main idea of paragraph A?
   A. Maria has injured herself.
   B. Pavement is not good for skateboarding.
   C. Maria is having difficulty learning a trick.
   D. Maria has given up trying to skateboard.

3. In paragraph F, what does Maria say to get Randall to see her point of view?

   _____

   _____

   _____

4. Which of the following supports that Randall has listened to Maria in paragraph G?
   A. He keeps on teasing her.
   B. He tells her how to fix what she is doing wrong.
   C. He tells her to watch what he is doing.
   D. He ignores her.

   Which three sentences are the best evidence? ____, ____, ____

5. From their dialog, you can tell that Maria and Randall:
   A. don't get along very well.
   B. are shy around one another.
   C. like to tease one another.
   D. don't have anything in common.

   Which three paragraphs are the best evidence? ____, ____, ____

DEFINING VOCABULARY USING CONTEXT

Using Context Clues Within the Sentence

When reading a story, you may see a word you don't know. How can you figure out what this new word means? You could try using context clues. **Context** is the other words, and sometimes other sentences, that help give a word meaning. Sometimes the context clues are in the same sentence. What does the word *adorned* mean?

A   The girls **adorned** their hair with flowers and ribbons.

Flowers and ribbons are clue words. You can guess that the girls *put* flowers and ribbons in their hair. So the word *adorned* probably means to decorate. Since they probably did this to make themselves look pretty, *adorned* could also mean to make something beautiful.

Sometimes the context clues describe the meaning of a word for you. Look at the following example.

B   Her **loquacious** friend nearly talked my ear off all evening.

The words *nearly talked my ear off* tell you that a loquacious person probably likes to talk a lot. Try to use another word or group of words with the same meaning in place of the first word. If *loquacious* means talks a lot or talkative, then replace it with the word *talkative*. Does the sentence still make sense? If it does, you are probably on the right track.

1.   Underline the words that describe the meaning of *renovate*.

C   Owners of old homes often **renovate** them, making them look exactly as they did when they were first built.

2.   Using context clues from the sentence, what do you think the word *disheveled* means in the next sentence?

_____

D   His **disheveled** hair looked as if a bird had tried to make a nest in it.

Practice Activity 1

Read the following sentence. Then read the first question and circle the letter of the correct answer.

My mother always kept her **equanimity,** even when the rest of the family were arguing and fighting with one another; she was our peacekeeper.

1. Which of the following words means almost the same as *equanimity*?

   A. angry mood

   B. calmness

   C. indifference

   D. anxiety

Look at the phrase *even when the rest of the family were arguing and fighting.* This phrase gives you a clue that mother acted differently from the rest of the family. The word *peacekeeper* also describes the mother's behavior. So which choice would make more sense, A or B? Try putting each word or phrase in place of the word *equanimity.* Look at choices C and D. Is either of these a better choice?

Practice Activity 2

Read the following sentence. Then read the question and circle the letter of the correct answer.

She spoke in such a low whisper that her voice was barely **audible,** and I had to bend down to hear her.

1. Which one of the following means almost the same as *audible*?

   A. soft

   B. heard

   C. spoken

   D. high

2. Which words in the sentence help you to figure out the meaning of *audible*?

_____

Using Context Clues From Other Sentences

Context clues can also be words in other sentences that help you figure out the meaning of a new word.

E   ¹Her brother was **voracious.** ²He was always eating. ³He could put away twice as much food as anyone else and still be hungry an hour later. ⁴He was never full.

The first sentence does not give any information about the word *voracious*. Sentence 2 gives a clue that it has to do with always eating. Sentences 3 and 4 then describe her brother's eating in greater detail. Using these clues, you can guess that the word *voracious* could mean always eating large amounts of food. Put these words in place of *voracious* in sentence 1 to see if the sentence still makes sense: Her brother was always eating large amounts of food.

Read the following paragraph then answer the question.

F   ¹She became more and more **introverted.** ²She stopped talking to her friends, even on the phone. ³She spent hours alone in her room. ⁴She just sat and read quietly, or sometimes just stared at her reflection in the mirror.

1.   Which one of the following words means almost the same as *introverted?*

   A.   outgoing

   B.   angry at everyone

   C.   focused on herself

   D.   excited

2.   Which words are context clues? _____

Sentence 1 tells you that a person was *introverted*. But it doesn't tell you what that person was like. You have to look at the other sentences to figure out the meaning of the word *introverted*.

Try putting *outgoing* in place of introverted in sentence 1. Now read sentence 2. Would she be more outgoing if she stopped talking to her friends?

Try putting *angry at everyone* in place of introverted. Read the rest of the sentences. Does this phrase make sense in the paragraph?

This leaves choices C and D. Which one makes the most sense in the paragraph?

The following key phrases give you clues about the meaning of introverted:

stopped talking to her friends, spent hours alone, stared at her reflection.

Practice Activity 3

Read the following paragraph then circle the correct answer.

¹The phone rang unexpectedly very early in the morning. ²It was a short call, but Uncle Art seemed **perturbed** after the call. ³He wouldn't talk to anyone. ⁴He just kept lighting one cigarette after another and pacing back and forth with a frown on his face.

1. Which of the following words means almost the same as *perturbed*?

   A. curious

   B. upset

   C. sad

   D. tired

2. Which clues in the other sentences help to support the answer?

   _____

   _____

Using Other Kinds of Context Clues

Other types of clues can help you define a word. Punctuation can be a clue. Look at the following sentence.

G   Herbivorous, or plant-eating, dinosaurs like the brontosaurus ate mainly leaves and grasses.

The commas in the sentence are a clue that the words between them describe the word *herbivorous*. In this case, the phrase *plant-eating* is given as a definition of herbivorous. The meaning of herbivorous is also supported by the fact that the brontosaurus ate leaves and grasses.

Other kinds of punctuation can also give clues. Parentheses ( ) can also be used to set apart words that give meaning to another word. An exclamation mark gives you a clue about a character's mood or feelings.

Other kinds of context clues that you can use are the title of the story, what the characters say and do, and even pictures.

Look at the example below.

1.   What clues are you given that the word railed means shouted?

H   "You won't get away with this!" the angry man **railed** at the children.

_____

_____

22. Corporal Vinny
by Mary-Ann Lucido

A [1]My name is Corporal Vinny, and I have trained my whole life for this hard job. [2]I must be able to swim in **turbulent** waters, no matter how rough. [3]I must be **agile** enough to climb steep cliffs and cross narrow ledges. [4]If I fall, I must be able to get back up right away and continue my journey. [5]I also must be able to outsmart my enemy so I don't get caught. [6]I'm a scout for the most important army in the world. [7]I'm the soldier who goes ahead of everyone else to find the food. [8]Crumbs of cake, sugar, candy, even crusts from a half-eaten sandwich can furnish many meals for my comrades.

B [9]Finding the food isn't the tricky part of the job, it's trying to find it *again* with the rest of the army in tow. [10]Once I found a yummy piece of fudge. [11]My eyes lit up like a Christmas tree. [12]I walked over and tried a tasty little **morsel**. [13]I had never tasted anything so good. [14]"Perfect!" I said out loud with a very satisfied smile on my face. [15]I began the long **trek** back to my platoon, which was waiting for me under the kitchen sink. [16]"Everyone follow me," I yelled.

[17]"I've found something delicious!" [18]They all gathered up their sleeping bags and canteens and started to follow me to the piece of fudge. [19]But I couldn't find it again. [20]We walked for hours. [21]Everyone was tired, and their feet were hurting. [22]The promise of that **delectable** fudge kept them going a lot longer than I thought they would. [23]But eventually they all started groaning and throwing their canteens and sleeping bags at me. [24]I felt awful. [25]I'm telling you, I never let that happen again. [26]Now when I find something, I drop pieces of salt on my way back to the guys. [27]My wife thinks I'm the smartest, bravest ant in the colony.

DIRECTIONS: Circle the letter next to the correct answer or write the answer on the lines given. When asked for evidence, write the number of the sentence or the letter of the paragraph that best supports the answer.

1. What does the word *turbulent* in sentence 2 mean?
   A. shallow
   B. deep
   C. unsettled
   D. flowing

   Which word in sentence 2 is the best context clue?

   _____

2. The word *agile* in sentence 3 means:
   A. awkward.
   B. athletic.
   C. careful.
   D. forceful.

3. In sentence 12, the word *morsel* most nearly means:
   A. sniff.
   B. feel.
   C. drink.
   D. bite.

   Which word in sentence 12 is the best context clue?

   _____

4. In sentence 15, a long *trek* is a:
   A. journey.
   B. visit.
   C. escape.
   D. slide.

   Which phrase in the sentence is the best context clue?

   _____

5. Which word could replace *delectable* in sentence 22?
   A. fattening
   B. delicious
   C. chocolate
   D. homemade

23. Dr. Robot
by M. A. Hockett

A [1]Let's say you are an astronaut in outer space. [2]You start getting pains and fever. [3]You must have your appendix taken out right away. [4]The nearest doctor is millions of miles away. [5]Will you die? [6]Not if you have a robot to do the operation!

B [7]This is no longer science fiction. [8]The first such **procedure** has been done. [9]"Operation Lindbergh" was successfully completed in September 2001. [10]In New York, Dr. Jacques Marescaux operated on the gallbladder* of a patient. [11]Not usually a big deal. [12]But this operation was done by **remote** control. [13]The woman was 4,000 miles away, in France!

C [14]How was this possible? [15]In New York, Dr. Marescaux **monitored** the patient by watching a screen. [16]He used **sensitive** tools, since every movement had to be detected. [17]The movements were then changed into signals. [18]The signals were sent across the Atlantic Ocean. [19]In France, a robot got the signals and made the same movements using operating tools.

D [20]Wasn't this a **hazardous** thing to try? [21]Not really. [22]Many steps had been taken for safety. [23]For one thing, doctors had practiced the operation on pigs. [24]Also, there were 80 people ready to help if something went wrong. [25]For another thing, the signal speed had been improved. [26]Pictures of the woman had to be fast so the doctor could always see what was happening. [27]The signals now took only about 150 **milliseconds** to travel from the robot to the doctor!

E [28]What about the woman in France? [29]The operation was a success! [30]She felt good, not only because her gallbladder was fixed. [31]She felt good about the part she played in making medical history.

*gallbladder: a sac, by the liver, that is used to hold fluid to help digestion

DIRECTIONS: Circle the letter next to the correct answer or write the answer on the lines given. When asked for evidence, write the number of the sentence or the letter of the paragraph that best supports the answer.

1. Which word in paragraph A means almost the same as *procedure*?
   A. appendix
   B. operation
   C. robot
   D. fever

2. What does the word *monitored* mean in sentence 15?
   A. gave medicine to
   B. spoke to
   C. moved tools
   D. kept track of

   Which other words in sentence 15 help give the meaning of *monitored*?

   _____

3. Which phrase best gives the meaning of *sensitive* as used in sentence 16?
   A. able to notice small changes
   B. seen on a screen
   C. very small in size
   D. used to create signals

4. What does the word *hazardous* mean, as used in sentence 20?

   _____

   Which other sentence is the best context clue? _____

5. As used in sentence 27, one *millisecond* is probably:
   A. about an hour.
   B. more than a minute.
   C. less than a second.
   D. a million seconds.

6. If you do something by *remote* (in sentence 12), you probably do it:
   A. by using robots.
   B. from a television.
   C. by using doctors.
   D. from a distance.

   Which sentence best supports your answer? _____

24. Sylvia Earle: Hero for the Ocean
by Christine Broz

A [1]Sylvia Earle is a hero for the ocean. [2]She is a marine biologist, explorer, and author. [3]She has devoted her life to the study and **conservation** of the underwater world. [4]Even though the ocean is huge, it still needs protection.

B [5]Earle is one of the world's best known marine biologists. [6]She first began to study sea life as a teenager. [7]She lived on the Florida coast with the ocean as her backyard. [8]Over the years, she has spent more than 6,000 hours diving to study the ocean and its life. [9]She has also helped other scientists gather information about sea life. [10]Earle has been the project director for a five-year study of the U.S. National Marine Sanctuaries. [11]Marine sanctuaries are protected areas of the ocean.

C [12]Earle has been called "Her Deepness" because she has gone on more than 50 underwater **expeditions** to explore some of the deep parts of the ocean. [13]In 1970, she was captain of the first team of women to live under the ocean for two weeks. [14]She currently holds the world record for a solo dive to 1,000 meters below the surface. [15]Her interest in and love for the ocean world **motivated** her to create a company to build deep sea vehicles for exploration.

D [16]Sylvia Earle is on a mission to share what she learns about the ocean. [17]She has written many books and articles about the ocean. [18]They detail the wonderful world of life present in the ocean, from vent worms to gray whales. [19]Her writing also tells of the damage humans have done to ocean **habitats** and of what needs to change if these underwater homes and the creatures that live there are to be saved. [20]She believes we will not work to save what we do not know exists.

E [21]Sylvia Earle is a strong **advocate** for the ocean. [22]Her work shows her support of keeping the oceans healthy for future generations. [23]Now in her mid-60s, Earle still has that childlike curiosity about the ocean. [24]This leads her to continue her explorations and inspire others to work to save the ocean.

DIRECTIONS: Circle the letter next to the correct answer or write the answer on the lines given. When asked for evidence, write the number of the sentence or the letter of the paragraph that best supports the answer.

1. Which word is closest in meaning to the word *conservation*?
   A. construction
   B. damage
   C. discussion
   D. protection

   Which other sentence gives the best context clue? _____

2. In paragraph C, what is the best word to replace *expeditions*?
   A. tests
   B. trips
   C. vacations
   D. contests

3. Which parts of sentence 12 help explain the meaning of the word *expeditions*?
   A. gone on
   B. to explore
   C. deep parts
   D. underwater

4. Which word can be used instead of the word *motivated* in sentence 15?
   A. prevented
   B. inspired
   C. designed
   D. forced

   Which words in sentence 15 are a context clue?

   _____

5. Write the part of sentence 19 that explains what the word *habitats* means.

   _____

   _____

6. What is the best meaning of the word *advocate,* as used in sentence 21?
   A. photographer
   B. councilor
   C. supporter
   D. deep-sea diver

   Which other sentence gives the best context clue? _____

USING FIGURATIVE LANGUAGE

What Is Figurative Language?

Writers use words to create an image in the reader's mind. Literal language uses the basic meaning of the words to describe something. **Figurative language** is words used in a creative way to describe something. Figurative language can describe something by comparing it to something similar. For example:

Literal: He looked strong.

Figurative: The muscles in his arms looked like bowling balls.

Of course, his arms are not really that big, but comparing them to bowling balls gives you an image of how strong he is. Figurative language uses your imagination to picture something.

Figurative language also uses words to mean something other than their dictionary or *literal* meaning.

Literal: Her constant lateness really annoyed me.

Figurative: Her constant lateness really got my goat.

Imagery

Imagery is the most common figurative language. **Imagery** uses your senses to suggest how something looks, feels, smell, sounds, or tastes.

Sight: The fall leaves <u>glowed bright red and gold</u>.

Sound: The dry leaves <u>crackled</u> under his feet.

Feel: The <u>velvety leaf</u> brushed against her cheek.

Smell: The <u>smoky scent</u> of <u>burning leaves</u> filled the air.

Taste: The <u>tart berry puckered</u> her lips.

1.   What kind of imagery is used below? _____

A   [1]The icy wind stung her face. [2]Tiny crystals caught in her lashes. [3]She could barely see through the blowing snow. [4]She pulled her scarf up higher.

Simile and Metaphor

Simile and metaphor are both types of figurative language used to compare two things.

> Simile: A comparison of two things using the word *like* or *as*.

> Metaphor: A comparison of two things which suggests that one thing *is* the other.

Look at the two examples below. Which one is a simile? Why?

A   1. She floated in the air like a feather.

      2. Her lined face was a map of her life.

Sentence one is a simile. It uses "like" to compare two things, a girl and a feather. It says she floated *like a feather*. Sentence two is a metaphor; it suggests that her face is a map.

Figurative language is used in the following paragraph to describe a young girl.

B   ¹She was the fairest flower in the garden. ²Her two lips formed a perfect rosebud. ³Her skin was as soft as a flower petal. ⁴She was perfect.

Identify which sentences use simile and which sentences use metaphor and write the sentence numbers on the lines.

Simile: _____   Metaphor: _____

Read the next paragraph.

C   ¹He felt her coldness towards him. ²Nothing he said could melt her frozen heart. ³It might as well have been a block of ice.

What kind of figurative language is used?

_____

Idioms

When you say, "My father blew his stack last night," you don't really mean that your father has a stack on his head or that he actually exploded. You mean he was angry. An **idiom** is a word or phrase in which the words used mean something different than their literal (dictionary) meaning. I "wash my hands of you" or he "lost track" of the time are examples of idioms. Underline the idioms in the next paragraph. What do you think each phrase means?

D ^{1}The teacher told the kids in the corner to quit horsing around. ^{2}It was time to buckle down and start working.

In sentence one, the phrase "horsing around" probably means playing noisily, like a herd of horses. "Buckle down" could mean get focused or pay attention.

The next paragraph has two idioms. Underline the idioms then explain what you think each one means.

E ^{1}George thought that Clint had taken the money. ^{2}I told him I thought he was barking up the wrong tree. ^{3}There wasn't any proof that it was Clint, and Clint was our friend. ^{4}But George was between a rock and a hard place. ^{5}Either lose a friend or lose his job.

Idiom 1 means:

_____

Idiom 2 means:

_____

Personification

Sometimes a writer will describe an object in human terms. This kind of figurative language is called personification. **Personification** is giving human qualities to nonliving things.

What is being personified in the next paragraph? _____

F   ¹I watch the daffodils poke their sleepy heads through the soil. ²In a matter of days, bright yellow daffodils are nodding cheerfully in the garden. ³Clusters of purple hyacinth stand at attention between them.

The next paragraph describes a microwave oven. Underline the examples of personification.

G   ¹Sometimes I'll be sitting here and everything is quiet and peaceful. ²But then somebody comes along and disturbs me. ³First, they open my door. ⁴Then they insert a big bowl of soup or a dish of spaghetti. ⁵They leave it in me, close the door, and poke my face a few times. ⁶That's kind of insulting.

What does "poke my face" in sentence 5 mean?

_____

25. *River* (Excerpt)
by Gary Paulsen

A [1]He was awakened by an explosion.

B [2]It seemed to come from inside his skull, inside his thinking, inside the dream: a sharp crack, so loud that he snapped awake, rolled over, and was on his feet, moving to the back of the shelter without thinking, without knowing he was moving.

C [3]It was thunder.

D [4]But not like he'd heard before, not like he'd ever heard. [5]It was around them, exploding around them, the lightning cracking around the shelter, so close it seemed to Brian that it came from inside him.

E [6]"What–"

F [7]He knew that he opened his mouth, that he made sound, but he could hear nothing except the *whack-crack* of the thunder, see nothing but images frozen in the split-instants of brilliance from the lightning.

G [8]Like a camera taking pictures by a strobe light, things would seem frozen in time, caught and frozen, and then there would be another flash and things would be different.

H [9]Derek was moving.

I [10]In one flash he was still on his bed, but raised, his jacket falling away from where he'd had it as a blanket, as he rose.

J [11]Darkness.

K [12]Then the next flash of light and he was on his knees.

L [13]Darkness.

M [14]Then he was leaning forward and his hand was out, reaching for his briefcase and radio next to the bed, one finger out, his face concentrating; and Brian thought, no, don't reach, stay low; and he might have yelled it, screamed it, but it didn't matter. [15]No sound could be loud enough to get over the thunder.

N [16]There was a slashing, new, impossibly loud crack as lightning seemed to hit the shelter itself and Brian saw the top of the pine next to the opening suddenly explode and felt/saw the bolt come roaring down the tree, burning and splitting and splintering the wood and bark, and he saw it hit Derek.

O [17]Camera image.

P [18]Some *thing*, some blueness of heat and light and raw power seemed to jump from the tree to the briefcase and radio and enter Derek's hand. [19]All in the same part of a second it hit him and his back arched, snapped him erect, and then it seemed to fill the whole shelter and slammed into Brian as well.

Q [20]He saw the blueness, almost a ball of energy, the crack/flash of color that came from inside his mind, inside his life, and then he was back and down and saw nothing more.

DIRECTIONS: Circle the letter next to the correct answer or write the answer on the lines given. When asked for evidence, write the number of the sentence or the letter of the paragraph that best supports the answer.

1. What type of figurative language does sentence 8 contain?
   A. imagery
   B. metaphor
   C. idiom
   D. simile

   What two things are being compared in this example?

   _____

   _____

2. What phrase is used to describe the sound the thunder made?

   _____

   Which sentence is the best evidence? _____

3. Which type of imagery is NOT used in sentence 16?
   A. sight
   B. smell
   C. sound
   D. feel

4. How does the author use figurative language to keep the plot moving?
   A. The sights and sounds of the storm are building up during the passage.
   B. Each paragraph contains another crash of thunder and a flash of lightning.
   C. The passage starts and ends with images of lightning.
   D. Each lightning flash shows a new action, like a series of photos.

5. What is described as a "ball of energy" in paragraph Q?
   A. the thunder
   B. the raw power
   C. the shelter
   D. the lightning

   Which sentence is the best evidence? _____

6. In sentence 7, what is meant by the words "images frozen"?

   _____

   _____

   _____

26. Sal and Dozer Don
by Mary-Ann Lucido

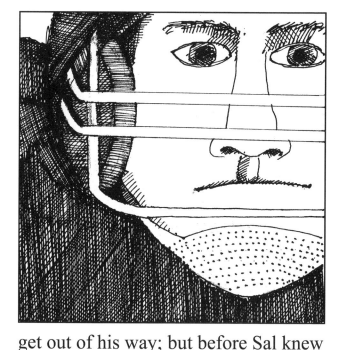

A [1]At 6 feet 1 inch, 200-pound Sal Lucy was one of the leading tacklers on the Monterey High School varsity football team. [2]Tonight his team was playing Seaside High School. [3]Now, to a crow flying by, the Seaside football players looked like any other ordinary varsity team. [4]But from the ground, you could see one anomaly—6-feet 6-inch, 350-pound Don Vera, fondly known as Dozer Don.

B [5]By the third quarter of the game, Sal had successfully avoided any contact with Dozer Don. [6]To tell the truth, Sal was afraid of him. [7]He had seen the destruction Dozer Don made on his way to a touchdown. [8]Sal didn't want to be one of the casualties. [9]But here he was in the third quarter of the game in a very precarious position. [10]The only thing between a touchdown and Dozer Don was Sal. [11]There was no question in Sal's mind, he was going to avoid this human steamroller at all costs. [12]Sal tried desperately to get out of his way; but before Sal knew what was happening they collided.

C [13]CRASH! CRUNCH! [14]Upon collision, Sal felt his body exploding like a 7 UP® can after it has been shaken. [15]He actually saw stars and heard birds while the announcer said, "Sal Lucy on that tackle." [16]Everyone was cheering. [17]Dozer Don helped Sal up. [18]"Good tackle, Kid."

D [19]While everyone was still cheering for him, a very disoriented Sal barely managed to walk back to the huddle— only it was the wrong huddle.

DIRECTIONS: Circle the letter next to the correct answer or write the answer on the lines given. When asked for evidence, write the number of the sentence or the letter of the paragraph that best supports the answer.

1. In sentence 4, what do you think the word *anomaly* means?
   A. something ordinary
   B. something awkward
   C. something unusual
   D. something mysterious

   Which other sentence gives the best evidence? _____

2. What do the words *precarious position* in sentence 9 mean?
   A. dangerous spot
   B. perfect position
   C. out of place
   D. defensive lineup

   Which sentence in paragraph B is an example of this? _____

3. What does Sal compare Don to in paragraph B?

   _____

   Which sentence is the best evidence? _____

   Explain what this comparison means.

   _____

   _____

   _____

4. Why does the author use the words *crash* and *crunch* in sentence 13?

   _____

   _____

   _____

5. What kind of figurative language is used in sentence 14?
   A. idiom
   B. metaphor
   C. simile
   D. personification

6. What does the word *disoriented* in sentence 19 mean?
   A. excited
   B. confused
   C. anxious
   D. annoyed

   Which phrase in sentence 19 gives context to support the meaning?

   _____

   _____

27. That's Gratitude for You
by M. A. Hockett

A ¹Mr. Grossman was one large math teacher, but that didn't slow him down. ²When he got excited about an equation, he was a tornado of flying chalks, eraser, and coattails! ³We would see one hand as a blur of motion against the board. ⁴The other hand would hold his toupee on his head, which you'd have to guess was somewhere on the other side of those huge shoulders. ⁵(He thought his head looked too small without the wig.) ⁶Next thing you knew, he'd be standing there, arms crossed, like a one-ton statue, as if he had never moved a muscle.

B ⁷Well, the big disaster happened at the school dance when it was Mr. Grossman's turn to chaperone. ⁸Everything went well for awhile. ⁹He spun Ms. Greer around, did a double turn himself, and caught Mrs. Hayward for a dip—all in one smooth motion. ¹⁰Then he gave his head a toss back before galloping across the floor like a wild colt.

C ¹¹What he didn't realize was that when he tossed his head, the toupee flew off! ¹²It went right over our heads and—plop!—into the punch bowl. ¹³Old Miss Pratt had looked away to say hello to Mr. Parker. ¹⁴She was looking at him as she lifted a dipperful of hair out of the bowl. ¹⁵Fortunately, when she looked back, the toupee had already fallen off the dipper and onto the floor.

D ¹⁶I had to get that toupee back for Mr. Grossman! ¹⁷I ran for the table, ducked down, and grabbed, but my hand came up empty! ¹⁸The hairpiece had a mind of its own. ¹⁹Somehow, it had scooted back onto the dance floor.

E ²⁰I scrambled for the wig through dozens of dancing legs that played soccer with it. ²¹I felt like I was playing keepaway with a giant centipede! ²²Each time I reached the hairpiece, another one of the legs gave it a slide or a shove.

F ²³Then it landed on a girl's foot, and she booted it up right in front of me. ²⁴I finally got my hands on it! ²⁵Mr. Grossman, who had been doing a duckwalk, popped up that very moment—right under the wig! ²⁶His eyebrows shot up in surprise. ²⁷"Foster, are you trying to steal my hairpiece?" he said. ²⁸He lowered his voice and continued, "You know I get embarrassed without it."

G ²⁹I stood with my mouth open as he adjusted his "hair" and then took another duckwalk across the room.

DIRECTIONS: Circle the letter next to the correct answer or write the answer on the lines given. When asked for evidence, write the number of the sentence or the letter of the paragraph that best supports the answer.

1. The metaphor in paragraph A compares Mr. Grossman to a:
   A. tornado.
   B. statue.
   C. wig.
   D. teacher.

   Which sentence has the metaphor? _____

2. Write the simile used in paragraph A.

   _____

3. What two things are being compared in the simile given in sentence 10?

   _____

   _____

4. The toupee is personified in what two sentences in paragraph D?

   _____, _____

   Write the phrases showing personification.

   _____

   _____

   _____

5. The metaphor in paragraph E compares the dancers to:
   A. many legs.
   B. a toupee.
   C. a centipede.
   D. a dance floor.

   Which two sentences are the best evidence? _____, _____

6. What does it mean that Mr. Grossman's eyebrows "shot up" in sentence 26? His eyebrows:
   A. flew off.
   B. rose quickly.
   C. slowly lifted.
   D. came together.

DETERMINING CAUSE AND EFFECT

What Is the Cause?

When something happens, you can usually find a reason for it. The **cause** of an event tells you *why* something happened. If you are late for school, the cause may be that you overslept or you missed the bus. When you read a story, you look for the causes of the events in the story.

Read the following story.

A   ¹Carly had been looking forward to seeing the play. ²When she got to the theater, the sign said the tickets were sold out. ³Since the tickets were sold out, Carly did not get to see the play.

Why wasn't Carly able to see the play? The tickets were sold out. The word *since* also helps to point out the cause.

It is important to make sure that one event really is the cause of another. While two events can happen at the same time, one event may not have directly caused the other. Read the following story.

B   ¹The cobra is a deadly snake. ²A cobra will lift its body to attack. ³Some cobras bite their prey with poisonous fangs. ⁴Other cobras squirt the poison in their prey's nose.

What causes the cobra to bite its prey? The answer is not really given in the paragraph. Lifting its body does not cause the cobra to bite. It may lift its body and not attack the prey. Lifting the body and biting may happen together, but one does not actually cause the other.

What Is the Effect?

The **effect** is a change that results from a cause. It tells us *what* happened as a result of something else. For example, "It started to rain on the day of the school picnic, so the picnic was cancelled." The effect was that the picnic was cancelled. The cause was the rain.

An event can have more than one effect. In the next paragraph, we learn about the effects of the storm before we find out the cause. What were the effects of the storm?

C   ¹Trees were blown down. ²Streets were flooded. ³Whole houses were lifted in the air. ⁴The damage was **caused by** a tornado that hit our town.

Effects: _____

_____

Read the next story.

D   ¹Shania had just finished the floor and was putting away the mop when Earl opened the door. ²"Wait," she cried, "Don't let him in." ³But it was too late. ⁴Scooter leaped over Earl's arm and raced across the floor, leaving a trail of muddy paw prints. ⁵Earl tore after him, leaving his own set of prints. ⁶When Shania looked at what they had done to her floor, she plopped down and started to cry.

1. What was the result of letting Scooter in the house?

_____

2. What effect did Earl and Scooter have on Shania?

_____

Looking for Signal Words

Certain key words can help you recognize whether an event is a cause or an effect. These words are called signal words.

Signal words that can show **cause**:

because	created by	the reason for	since
caused by	led to	on account of	due to

Signal words that can show **effect**:

therefore	then	as a result	thus
finally	so		

In each of the sentences below, identify the cause and the effect. Look for signal words to help you.

		Cause	**Effect**
1.	Since it was getting dark, he went home.	it was getting dark	he went home
2.	A strike by the workers led to a safer place to work.		
3.	Their empty gas tank finally brought them to a stop.		
4.	Jim stayed home because he was afraid to fly.		
5.	Mother wasn't home yet, so we couldn't go outside to play.		
6.	The reason for Luis missing the bus was he got up late.		

Recognizing a Series of Causes

Sometimes there can be a sequence of causes for an event. One event causes the next event, which causes the next event, and so on. Look at the story below. What caused the soup to spill?

A   [1]Tia opened the door suddenly. [2]When it hit Mr. Cho, he tripped. [3]The bowl went flying out of his hands. [4]The bowl came crashing down. [5]Soup spilled all over the floor.

In this case, a series of events caused the soup to spill. The door opening caused Mr. Cho to trip. His tripping caused the bowl to fly out of his hands. The soup spilled when the bowl crashed down.

When no signal words are given, you have to read carefully to find the cause of an event. In the story above, there is an order that ties one event to the next.

Cause and Effect Practice Activity

Read the following story. Then answer the question.

¹A young boy fell into the gorilla's exhibit at the zoo. ²The crowd panicked because the gorilla picked up the boy! ³As the crowd watched, the gorilla carried the boy to the cage door. ⁴Zookeepers then reached in and pulled the boy out.

1. What caused the crowd to panic?

_____

Write the signal word that helped you find the answer.

_____

Sentence 2 tells you that the crowd panicked because <u>the gorilla picked up the boy</u>. The signal word **because** gives you a clue.

Read the next story and answer the question.

¹Lupe slowly sips Rani's new recipe for soup. ²It causes her face to turn bright red. ³Her eyes water. ⁴Finally she gasps for air.

⁵"Too much pepper?" asks Rani.

2. What effect does sipping Rani's soup have on Lupe?

_____

_____

_____

Sipping the soup results in a series of effects.

Which three sentences best support the answer? ____, ____, ____

28. Flash Flood
by Christine Broz

A [1]We had been waiting all summer for this hiking vacation through the canyons of Utah. [2]It had rained all through the night, but the sky was clearing. [3]We made our way down to the trail at the mouth of the canyon. [4]We signed in and hit the trail.

B [5]I remembered learning in school how these deep canyons were the result of water eroding the soft rock away. [6]Boulders and trees swept along with the rushing water had helped to carve the edges of the canyon. [7]The canyon walls were magnificent, rising hundreds of feet straight up.

C [8]A shallow river flowed slowly through the canyon at this time of year. [9]We thought the ankle-deep water was refreshingly cool. [10]The further we went into the canyon the narrower it became. [11]After an hour of hiking, we were in knee-deep water. [12]We climbed up to a ledge about fifteen feet above the water to take a break. [13]When we entered the water again in the same spot, it was up to our waists. [14]We knew something was wrong, so we scrambled back up to the ledge. [15]Nervously, we watched as the water continued to rise toward us. [16]Then it started coming in waves. [17]There was no way to climb any higher since the canyon walls went straight up. [18]We were trapped!

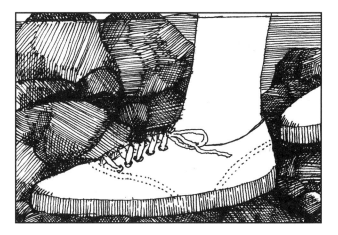

D [19]A short while later, we heard shouting. [20]It was hard to tell where it was coming from because the sound kept bouncing off the canyon walls. [21]Then we saw someone waving to us from the top of the canyon wall. [22]Thank goodness we had signed in so someone knew we were here. [23]The next thing we knew, a rope was swinging down toward us. [24]Finally we were pulled up to safety.

E [25]The ranger who rescued us said flash floods can happen anywhere downstream of a storm. [26]That morning the storm had moved off to the east but was continuing to rain down on areas upstream from this canyon. [27]Most of the water flowed down through the canyon. [28]The river picked up speed and depth where the canyon narrowed.

F [29]When we peered back over the edge of the canyon, all we saw was raging water. [30]My heart beat faster when I realized the ledge where we had been was now underwater. [31]Because of the flood, the canyon would be different after today.

DIRECTIONS: Circle the letter next to the correct answer or write the answer on the lines given. When asked for evidence, write the number of the sentence or the letter of the paragraph that best supports the answer.

1. What caused the canyons to form?
   A. water
   B. wind
   C. hikers
   D. falling rocks

   Which sentence is the best evidence? _____

2. In sentence 14, why did the hikers return to the ledge?
   A. They were still tired.
   B. They didn't want to get wet.
   C. The water had gotten deeper.
   D. There were boulders in the water.

   Which two sentences are the best evidence? _____, _____

3. In paragraph C, what kept the hikers from climbing higher?
   A. the rain
   B. the ranger
   C. the deep water
   D. the steep walls

   Which word is a signal word for the cause?

   _____

4. In paragraph D, why couldn't the hikers hear where the shouting was coming from?
   A. The river was too loud.
   B. The shouting was not loud enough.
   C. The sound echoed off the canyon walls.
   D. They were not listening hard enough.

   Which sentence is the best evidence? _____

5. The flood in the canyon was due to:

   _____

   _____

   Which paragraph is the best evidence? _____

6. What effect would this latest flood have on the canyon? It would make it:
   A. deeper and wider.
   B. shallower and narrower.
   C. have more trees.
   D. have no water.

   Which paragraph is the best evidence? _____

29. Getting the Job
by Cheryl Block

A [1]A good job interview can help you get the job you want. [2]Therefore, it's important to prepare for an interview ahead of time.

B [3]First impressions are important. [4]Research has shown that people can make up their minds about someone in the first five minutes of meeting them.

C [5]Follow some of these rules to make a good first impression:

D [6]Be on time. [7]Early is good, too. [8]Being on time shows that you are dependable. [9]Don't be late because they may think you are not that serious about the job.

E [10]Be neat and clean. [11]How you dress is important, too. [12]You don't want to look sloppy. [13]Don't dress up too much, either. [14]This is a job interview, not a date.

F [15]Be positive and relaxed. [16]This may not be easy. [17]Try to think of the interview as a conversation. [18]However, that doesn't mean you should talk to the interviewer in the same way you would talk with your friends.

G [19]Be prepared. [20]Bring important information with you so you are ready to answer any specific questions the interviewer may have. [21]This information could include a list of other jobs you have had, names of references, extra courses you've taken, volunteer work you've done, special skills you have, even samples of things you have done. [22]Having this information with you will make you better prepared for the interview.

H [23]Find out about the job and the company ahead of time. [24]What skills does the job require? [25]Then you can make a connection between your skills and the needs of the employer. [26]Remember, there are people skills as well as technical skills. [27]Being polite and friendly is just as important for a salesclerk as knowing how to use a cash register.

I [28]Go into your job interview positive and prepared. [29]A little planning ahead could just get you the job!

DIRECTIONS: Circle the letter next to the correct answer or write the answer on the lines given. When asked for evidence, write the number of the sentence or the letter of the paragraph that best supports the answer.

1. Why are first impressions important?

   _____

   _____

   Which sentence is the best evidence? _____

2. Being late to an interview could cause an employer to think you:
   A. don't pay attention.
   B. need to get a new watch.
   C. do not really want the job.
   D. are a dependable person.

   Which sentence is the best evidence? _____

3. Bringing important information with you will result in:
   A. making you better prepared to answer questions.
   B. making you look organized.
   C. keeping you busy.
   D. letting you tell all about yourself.

   Which sentence is the best evidence? _____

   Which word in the sentence signals the effect?

   _____

4. Finding out about the job ahead of time will help you to:
   A. ask for a higher salary.
   B. know where else to look for a job.
   C. develop your people skills.
   D. match your skills to the job.

   Which sentence is the best evidence? _____

30. A Wad of Gum
by Cheryl Block

A ¹It was all because of the gum. ²I forgot to spit it out before I went into math class. ³We had a new sub that morning, Miss Fine. ⁴When Miss F saw me chewing, she told me to spit it out. ⁵So I did. ⁶It was a clear shot from my desk to the trash can. ⁷But just as I let it fly, Serena stood up. ⁸Instead of landing in the trash can, the gum hit the back of her head and stuck to her hair.

B ⁹Serena squealed and tried to pull it out, but the big wad of gum just stuck harder. ¹⁰Then Serena started yelling at me and pulling at her hair. ¹¹So Manny grabbed the scissors off Miss F's desk to help Serena out. ¹²But Miss Fine, seeing the scissors in Manny's hand and being new, panicked and hit the security button on her desk. ¹³The school officer came running in the door as the alarm blared. ¹⁴Seeing Serena flailing and yelling as Manny approached her with the scissors, the guard assumed the worst and threw Manny to the floor.

C ¹⁵While Manny was yelling at the officer to get off him, Serena suddenly jerked the wad of gum free and threw it at me. ¹⁶It flew from her hand and hit Miss Fine in the side of the head. ¹⁷Miss F was so startled, she fell to the floor in a dead faint. ¹⁸Half the class whipped out their cell phones and starting calling 911.

D ¹⁹Meanwhile, the officer was now stretched out on the floor trying to revive Miss F while still holding down Manny. ²⁰I tried to explain to him about the gum, but he wasn't listening. ²¹I knew it was all over when Vice Principal Michin stormed into the room and hauled Manny and me to his office.

E ²²Which led to my present situation. ²³Let me tell you, gum duty is no picnic. ²⁴People find some pretty weird places to stick it!

DIRECTIONS: Circle the letter next to the correct answer or write the answer on the lines given. When asked for evidence, write the number of the sentence or the letter of the paragraph that best supports the answer.

1. Why was the narrator chewing gum in class?

   _____

   Which sentence is the best evidence? _____

2. Getting gum in her hair caused Serena to:
   A. stand up.
   B. start yelling.
   C. faint.
   D. panic.

   Which sentence is the best evidence? _____

3. The school officer threw Manny to the floor because:
   A. he didn't like his attitude.
   B. he thought Manny was attacking Serena.
   C. he thought Manny was attacking the teacher.
   D. he wanted to stop Serena's squealing.

   Which sentence is the best evidence? _____

4. Miss Fine fainted as a result of:
   A. being injured.
   B. being surprised.
   C. having a headache.
   D. all of the noise.

   Which sentence is the best evidence? _____

5. The chewing gum incident may have resulted in:
   A. gum being banned from school.
   B. the narrator getting cleanup duty.
   C. the narrator being put on detention.
   D. the school being closed.

   Which sentence is the best evidence? _____

   Which signal words are a clue?

   _____

31. Animal Eyes
by Cheryl Block

A [1]Not all animal eyes are the same. [2]They can vary in size, position, and use. [3]Animals that hunt at night often have extra big eyes to let in more light. [4]The tarsier* has the largest eyes of any animal its size. [5]It can see more easily in the dark than other animals. [6]Its eyes are so big, however, that they do not move. [7]The tarsier must turn its head around instead. [8]It can turn its head 180 degrees and look behind itself!

B [9]Most predators** have eyes that face forward. [10]Because the two eyes are close, they work together to focus more easily on prey. [11]Cats and owls have eyes in the front. [12]Most plant-eaters, such as deer and rabbits, have eyes farther apart on the sides of their heads. [13]These eyes let the animal look in all directions to watch for predators, but it is harder for the eyes to work together. [14]Some lizards have an eye on each side that can move independently of one another. [15]They can look in two different directions at the same time!

C [16]Most insects have compound eyes. [17]A compound eye is made up of hundreds of tiny single eyes grouped together. [18]Each single eye has its own lens and sees only part of an image. [19]Each eye also points in a slightly different direction, so each sees a different piece of the image. [20]The insect looks at all these pieces at the same time. [21]It's probably like looking through a kaleidoscope. [22]The many little eyes of the compound eye, however, can detect the slightest motion.

D [23]As you can see, there's a lot of variety in animal eyes. [24]Each animal's eyes are adapted to fit its needs.

*tarsier—a small, nocturnal mammal

**predator—an animal that hunts other animals for food

DIRECTIONS: Circle the letter next to the correct answer or write the answer on the lines given. When asked for evidence, write the number of the sentence or the letter of the paragraph that best supports the answer.

1. A larger eye helps an animal to see at night because it:
   A. lets the animal see a wider area.
   B. increases the amount of light to the eye.
   C. can move in more directions.
   D. can make objects seem larger.

   Which sentence is the best evidence? _____

2. Because eyes on the sides of the head are far apart, they do not

   _____

   Which two sentences are the best evidence? ____, ____

3. Because a plant-eater can see in many directions, it can:
   A. find food more easily.
   B. avoid being eaten.
   C. avoid flying insects.
   D. find other plant-eaters.

   Which sentence is the best evidence? _____

4. An insect sees an image in pieces because:
   A. each smaller eye sees separately.
   B. it looks at all the pieces at the same time.
   C. it has a kaleidoscope for an eye.
   D. each eye points in different directions.

   Which two sentences are the best evidence? _____, _____

5. Why do animals' eyes differ?

   _____

   _____

   _____

32. Rubber Roads
by M. A. Hockett

A [1]Your car rolls on just four rubber tires, right? [2]Maybe not. [3]On some highways, you may roll on millions of rubber tires! [4]That's because rubber tires are used in a special kind of pavement. [5]Each lane of this pavement may include 2,000 old tires per mile!

B [6]California, Arizona, and Texas use a special kind of rubber road pavement called Asphalt Rubber, or A-R. [7]To make A-R, asphalt cement is heated and mixed with rubber. [8]Rubber makes up at least 15% of the weight of the mix.

C [9]Using A-R in our roads helps get rid of heaps of used tires dotting our lands. [10]These old tires cause many problems. [11]For one thing, the tires attract mosquitoes, and mosquitoes are known to spread disease. [12]Burning tires causes air pollution, and the fires are hard to put out. [13]Burying tires is a problem because they easily rise to the surface and bring up other waste with them. [14]Using the old tires in our roads can help solve these problems.

D [15]There are many other benefits of using A-R. [16]Driving on A-R is not as noisy as on regular roads. [17]Because of this, sound walls can be smaller, and the cost of building sound walls is less. [18]A-R is applied in a thin layer, so it costs less than regular pavement for the same amount of road. [19]Also, since rubber is flexible, the road is less likely to crack and will last longer.

E [20]As you can see, driving on rubber makes sense—in more ways than one!

DIRECTIONS: Circle the letter next to the correct answer or write the answer on the lines given. When asked for evidence, write the number of the sentence or the letter of the paragraph that best supports the answer.

1. What cause is given for air pollution?
   A. tires rising to the surface
   B. smog from cars
   C. tires burning
   D. using rubber tires in the road

   Which sentence is the best evidence? _____

2. Some buried garbage ends up above ground because it is:
   A. dug up when people pull up tires.
   B. pulled along by rising tires.
   C. left over from making A-R.
   D. lighter than the tires.

   Which sentence is the best evidence? _____

3. Which of the following is an effect of using A-R?
   A. roads made completely of rubber
   B. increased piles of old tires
   C. spread of disease by mosquitoes
   D. reduced cost of paving roads

   Which two sentences are the best evidence for your answer?

   _____, _____

4. Find the cause and effect in sentence 19 and write them below.

   Cause _____

   _____

   Effect _____

   _____

   Write the signal word _____

5. According to paragraph D, why does it cost less to build sound walls?

   _____

   _____

   Which signal word is a clue to the answer? _____

33. "The Path of Our Sorrow"
from *Out of the Dust* (Excerpt)
by Karen Hesse

[1]Miss Freeland said,
[2]"During the Great War we fed the world.
[3]We couldn't grow enough wheat
[4]to fill all the bellies.
[5]The price the world paid for our wheat
[6]was so high,
[7]it swelled our wallets
[8]and our heads,
[9]and we bought bigger tractors,
[10]more acres,
[11]until we had mortgages
[12]and rent
[13]and bills
[14]beyond reason,
[15]but we all felt so useful, we didn't
      notice.
[16]Then the war ended and before long,
[17]Europe didn't need our wheat anymore,
[18]they could grow their own.
[19]But we needed Europe's money
[20]to pay our mortgage,
[21]our rent,
[22]our bills.
[23]We squeezed more cattle,
[24]more sheep
[25]onto less land
[26]and they grazed down the stubble
[27]till they reached root.
[28]And the price of wheat kept dropping

[29]so we had to grow more bushels
[30]to make the same amount of money we
      made before,
[31]to pay for all that equipment, all that
      land,
[32]and the more sod we plowed up,
[33]the drier things got,
[34]because the water that used to collect
      there
[35]under the grass,
[36]biding its time,
[37]keeping things alive through the dry
      spells
[38]wasn't there anymore.
[39]Without the sod the water vanished,
[40]the soil turned to dust.
[41]Until the wind took it,
[42]lifting it up and carrying it away.
[43]Such a sorrow doesn't come suddenly,
[44]there are a thousand steps to take
[45]before you get there."
[46]But now,
[47]sorrow climbs up our front steps,
[48]big as Texas, and we didn't even see it
      coming,
[49]even though it'd been making its way
      straight for us
[50]all along.

September 1934

DIRECTIONS: Circle the letter next to the correct answer or write the answer on the lines given. When asked for evidence, write the number of the sentence or the letter of the paragraph that best supports the answer.

1. In line 5, because wheat was selling for a high price, the farmers:
   A. cooked food for people around the world.
   B. raised more cattle and sheep.
   C. joined the military.
   D. bought more land and equipment.

   Which two other lines are the best evidence? ____, ____

2. The fact that Europe could grow its own wheat meant that:
   A. the world was no longer hungry.
   B. Europe stopped buying our wheat.
   C. wheat became more valuable.
   D. Europe had more money.

   Which line is the best evidence?

   ____

3. After the war, the farmers had to grow *more* wheat in line 29 because:
   A. the price of wheat went up.
   B. they needed to buy more tractors.
   C. the price of wheat was dropping.
   D. they needed to use more land.

   Which two lines are the best evidence? ____, ____

   Which word in line 29 is a signal word? _____

4. Put in the correct sequence the series of events that resulted in the land turning to dust:
   __ They plowed up more sod.
   __ The soil turned to dust.
   __ The wind blew the soil away.
   __ The sod dried up.

PREDICTION

Making Predictions

When reading a story, you often make predictions. A **prediction** is really a guess that you make about what will happen next using as much information as possible. The more information you have, the more likely your prediction is correct. When you try to predict how someone is going to act, you base your prediction on that character's traits and past actions. How has he or she behaved in the past that will give you a clue about future behavior? What will this character probably do this time? Read the following story.

A   ¹Uncle George was a huge man. ²He was so big he was almost scary. ³But he was the kindest soul I ever knew. ⁴He was always helping people. ⁵If someone needed a hand, he could count on Uncle George. ⁶He had never said no to anyone.

What do you think Uncle George would do if someone asked for a favor?

_____

Predicting Outcomes

When you predict the ending, or outcome, of a story, you should base your predictions on what has happened so far in the story. What do you already know about the characters and their actions? Do you think their behavior will change? Use evidence from the story to make your prediction. In the following story, can you predict what Gloria will do?

B   ¹Gloria slowly climbed the steps. ²She didn't want to try the ride. ³It was too high, too fast, too scary. ⁴Eddie said she was being a baby, but she didn't care. ⁵She just didn't like roller coasters, even though she hadn't been on one. ⁶She let the people behind her go ahead. ⁷Just watching the cars was making her dizzy. ⁸That made up her mind.

We know that Gloria doesn't like roller coasters and doesn't want to ride this one. She hasn't ever ridden one. Since she is getting dizzy just looking at the ride, and she let the people go in front of her, she probably won't ride.

34. Mind's Eye
by M. A. Hockett

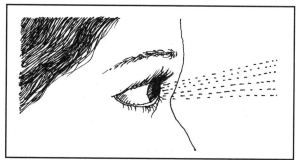

A [1]"Ready, Sarah?" Jominy, the transport control officer, asked.

B [2]Under my scalp was an amazing piece of new technology. [3]The Mind Control unit had been successfully implanted, but there was one catch. [4]It was not tested. [5]Melba, the ship's scientist, needed two weeks. [6]We didn't have two weeks. [7]We didn't have an hour.

C [8]A fleet of Too-Fee attack ships was headed for Earth. [9]The MC was our only chance to save the planet. [10]It worked only at close range, so I had to board their command ship.

D [11]"All set," I told Jominy. [12]In an instant, my body materialized on the alien ship.

E [13]"Stop right there!" a Too-Fee yelled, reaching for her stun stick. [14]"Relax and take me to your captain," I thought, looking into her eyes. [15]She lowered her weapon and did as I said.

F [16]I took care of each Too-Fee we passed. [17]The sooner I made eye contact, the sooner I could control their actions. [18]"Piece of cake!" I thought. [19]Melba's fear that enemy thoughts might backfeed into the MC and control *me* didn't seem to be a problem.

G [20]We reached the control room.

H [21]"Squadron, assume position and stand by for countdown...," said the commander. [22]Time was running out! [23]I would have to catch his eye and focus. [24]When he turned, my heart sank. [25]He was wearing a one-way visor! [26]I could not see his eyes.

I [27]Gaining control would take more time and effort than I had planned. [28]"But I can do it!" I thought. [29]Then I felt myself turn away and sit down. [30]"What am I doing?" I thought. [31]Then it hit me. [32]My lack of eye contact gave the commander time to *think* me into doing nothing.

J [33]Scenes of home ran through my mind. [34]Home, where justice prevailed, where happiness lived, where innocent friends awaited our return. [35]I had to save them! [36]I felt my passion overcoming his thoughts.

K [37]I got up, grabbed the visor, and tore it off. [38]The commander was stunned as I looked deep into his eyes and thought, "You will turn this ship around. [39]You will order the squadron back to your planet. [40]You will never bother us again." [41]Like a robot, he did as I ordered.

L [42]Back on my ship, I was welcomed as a hero. [43]Melba wanted my suggestions for improving the MC. [44]"Fix that backfeed problem," I said. [45]"Oh, and you might want to add a feature for x-ray vision."

DIRECTIONS: Circle the letter next to the correct answer or write the answer on the lines given. When asked for evidence, write the number of the sentence or the letter of the paragraph that best supports the answer.

1. In paragraph E, if Sarah had not had the MC unit, the Too-Fee would probably have:
   A. used her stun stick.
   B. used her laser gun.
   C. given Sarah a tour.
   D. given Sarah directions.

2. If the Earthlings had three weeks before they needed to use the MC, they probably would have:
   A. found someone else to use it.
   B. stopped the attack another way.
   C. used two weeks for testing it.
   D. found out that it was useless.

   Which two sentences are the best evidence? _____, _____

3. In paragraph I, Sarah predicted that she would need extra time to control the commander. She based this prediction on the fact that:
   A. the MC unit was untested.
   B. the Too-Fees were all difficult to control.
   C. he was about to attack Earth.
   D. control was quicker with eye contact.

   Which other paragraph is the best evidence? _____

4. What <u>probably</u> would have happened to Earth if Sarah had not been able to use the Mind Control unit?

   _____

   _____

   Which two sentences are the best evidence? _____, _____

5. In sentence 45, Sarah predicts that having x-ray vision will probably help her:
   A. see the eyes of someone she wants to control.
   B. contact the ship when she needs something.
   C. find the right people to control.
   D. see where she is going.

35. It's in the Dough
by Cheryl Block

A [1]Making your own pizza can be fun *and* educational. [2]Think of it as a science project you can eat. [3]For one thing, pizza dough uses yeast. [4]Yeast is a living fungus used in baking to ferment the dough. [5]Yeast needs warmth and moisture to start growing. [6]It feeds on sugar. [7]Fermentation is a process in which yeast breaks down the sugar in grain. [8]Since flour has only a small amount of natural sugar in it, bakers often add sugar. [9]As the yeast digests, it gives off tiny bubbles of carbon dioxide. [10]These bubbles inflate, causing the dough to expand, or rise. [11]The gas bubbles are trapped in the dough by a substance called *gluten*. [12]Gluten makes dough stretchy, like bubble gum. [13]Salt helps strengthen the gluten so the bubbles don't expand too quickly and burst.

B [14]The following recipe makes enough dough for two large pizzas.

Pizza Dough*

- 2 packages yeast
- 2 teaspoons sugar
- 4 cups flour (or more)
- 1 teaspoon salt
- 1/4 cup olive oil
- 1 and 1/2 cups warm water

Directions

C [15]Put yeast and sugar in a cup. [16]Add 1/2 cup of water. [17]The water should be warm not hot. [18]Mix well. [19]Wait about 5 minutes for the yeast to activate.

D [20]In a large mixing bowl, add the flour, salt, olive oil, 1 cup of warm water, and the yeast mixture. [21]Mix with a fork to get all the liquid absorbed by the flour.

E [22]Spread flour on a flat surface and dust your hands with it. [23]Pour the contents of the bowl on to the floured surface.

F [24]Knead the dough for 8–10 minutes or until the texture is smooth and even. [25]If the dough seems sticky, add a little more flour. [26]One way to knead is to lean on the dough with the palm of your hand and press down. [27]Fold the dough and repeat. [28]Kneading builds gluten.

G [29]Place dough in a bowl and drizzle with olive oil. [30]Place bowl in draft-free area and cover with a cloth.

H [31]Let the dough rise for about an hour. [32]Punch down the dough and wait about 45 minutes. [33]Your dough is now ready.

I [34]Cut the dough in half.

J [35]Dust a rolling pin with flour and roll out the dough on a floured surface until it is the desired shape. [36]Keep using flour so the dough doesn't stick.

K [37]Dust a cookie sheet with corn meal.

L [38]Use a spatula and slide the dough onto the cookie sheet. [39]Add your toppings and bake at 500° for 10–14 minutes.

*recipe courtesy of www.pizzatherapy.com

DIRECTIONS: Circle the letter next to the correct answer or write the answer on the lines given. When asked for evidence, write the number of the sentence or the letter of the paragraph that best supports the answer.

1. Predict what will happen if you make pizza using cold water.
   A. It won't make a difference.
   B. The yeast will grow more quickly.
   C. The dough won't rise.
   D. The dough will be more elastic.

   Which three sentences are the best evidence? ____, ____, ____

2. What will happen if you forget to flour the surface before kneading the dough?

   _____

   Which sentence is the best evidence? ____

3. Predict what will happen if you leave out the sugar.
   A. The yeast won't ferment.
   B. The dough won't rise as quickly.
   C. The dough will be too thick.
   D. The pizza will be too salty.

4. Predict what happens if dough doesn't rise.
   A. It has no effect on the bread.
   B. The bread has a heavy texture.
   C. The dough remains sticky.
   D. The pizza will take longer to bake.

5. What will baking the dough do to the yeast? It will:
   A. keep growing.
   B. be killed.
   C. change to sugar.
   D. burst.

6. Predict what leaving out the salt will do.
   A. The bread will rise too much.
   B. The bread may be too sweet.
   C. The dough won't rise as much.
   D. The yeast won't ferment.

   Which sentence is the best evidence? ____

DETERMINING FACT AND OPINION

Is It Fact or Opinion?

It is important to be able to tell the difference between facts and opinions when making decisions or drawing conclusions. A **fact** is a statement that can be proven based on evidence.

A   Hawaii is a group of islands in the Pacific Ocean.
        (You can check a map.)

An **opinion** is a view of something that cannot be proven true or false. It is often what someone thinks or believes but cannot prove.

B   I think Hawaii is the best place to go for a vacation.
        (There is no way to prove this because people have different ideas about what is a good vacation.)

Look for words like *think* and *believe*. Value words like *best, worst, terrific, beautiful, lots,* etc., can also help you to identify opinions. Read the following and decide which sentences are facts and which are opinions.

C   ¹I saw a science fiction movie last night. ²It was a terrific movie! ³It was about aliens covered with green scales invading Earth. ⁴The aliens looked really ugly. ⁵There was lots of exciting action. ⁶There were three battle scenes between the alien spaceships and the Earthlings.

Sentence 1 is a fact. You can check if someone went to the movies and what kind of movie it was. Sentence 2 is an opinon. *Terrific* is a value word that gives someone's personal view of the movie. Sentence 3 is a fact; the plot and characters of the movie can be checked. Sentence 4 is an opinion.

1. Is sentence 5 a fact or an opinion?   F   O

2. Which words helped you decide? _____

3. Is sentence 6 a fact or an opinion?   F   O

4. Explain why _____

36. Bubblemania

by Christine Broz

A [1]Many people enjoy chewing gum. [2]It has been around since the days of the ancient Mayans and Greeks. [3]But the best kind of gum to chew is bubble gum. [4]This pink sensation popped into existence in the early 1900s and continues to be popular.

B [5]Bubble gum was first invented by Frank Fleer in 1906. [6]However, it was too sticky to enjoy, and he didn't sell very much. [7]Then in 1928, twenty-three-year-old Walter Diemer, an accountant for Fleer's gum company, came up with a new recipe. [8]The new pink gum was stretchy and not as sticky as regular chewing gum. [9]Diemer was soon selling lots of it and teaching sales clerks how to blow bubbles. [10]Today, most bubble gum is the same playful pink color and comes in a variety of shapes.

C [11]People of all ages think bubble gum is fun. [12]Youngsters love the challenge of blowing bubbles the size of a grapefruit. [13]Some adults like it just because it reminds them of their childhood. [14]You are sure to feel silly when a huge bubble pops and sticks to your nose.

D [15]Bubble gum has been the subject of many contests and records. [16]Susan Montgomery Williams of California set a world record in 1994 for blowing a twenty-three-inch bubble. [17]People make up their own contests. [18]They compete for who can blow the biggest or fastest bubble. [19]They compete for who can blow the most bubbles in a minute, or bubbles that won't pop on their face before they can suck them back in. [20]They have found other amusing things to do with bubble gum. [21]These include blowing bubbles inside their mouths, inside a glass of soda, at the end of a straw, or with their noses.

E [22]Even the names of bubble gums are amusing. [23]The first bubble gum was called Blibber-Blubber. [24]Walter Diemer's gum was called Dubble Bubble. [25]In the 1930s, Bazooka® bubble gum was named after a funny looking musical instrument. [26]Then came Bubblicious®, Bubble Yum, and Hubba Bubba. [27]Try saying those names fast five times without cracking a smile.

F [28]Millions of pieces of bubble gum are chewed every year. [29]No wonder Walter Diemer was proud to say he made children happy all over the world.

DIRECTIONS: Circle the letter next to the correct answer or write the answer on the lines given. When asked for evidence, write the number of the sentence or the letter of the paragraph that best supports the answer.

1. Is sentence 3 a fact or an opinion?

   _____

   Which word in the sentence is a clue? _____

2. Which word in sentence 12 tells you this sentence is an opinion?

   _____

3. From paragraph B, list three facts about Walter Diemer's gum.

   _____

   _____

   _____

4. Label the following statements as F for fact or O for opinion.
   __ Bubble gum comes in a variety of shapes.
   __ The names of bubble gums are amusing.
   __ People have bubble gum contests.
   __ It is fun when a big bubble pops on your face.

5. Circle the letter next to the statements that are opinions.
   A. Walter Diemer was not the first person to make bubble gum.
   B. Millions of pieces of bubble gum are chewed each year.
   C. Bubblicious® and Hubba Bubba are funny bubble gum names.
   D. Good bubble gum is not sticky.

6. Which one of the following statements below can be proven?
   A. All bubble gum is fun.
   B. Bubble gum is silly.
   C. Bubble gum tastes better than chewing gum.
   D. Bazooka® bubble gum came before Bubblicious®.

   Which two sentences are the best evidence? ____, ____

37. Foods as Medicine
by Cheryl Block

A [1]We know that food provides us with nutrition and vitamins. [2]Scientists are now studying and testing claims that certain foods, called "functional foods," may also help to reduce the risk of disease if they are eaten regularly.

B [3]One group of functional foods is fruits and vegetables. [4]Scientists have found that tomatoes and broccoli contain natural chemicals that may help to fight disease.

C [5]Another group of functional foods is whole grains, like oat bran. [6]However, most people don't eat oat bran by itself. [7]Instead, oat bran is put into products such as oatmeal and certain breads. [8]Scientists have found strong evidence that eating oat bran can lower cholesterol. [9]Doctors have linked high levels of cholesterol to heart disease.

D [10]In 1997, the FDA (Food and Drug Administration) gave the Quaker Oats Company the first officially approved health claim for a food. [11]The FDA allowed the company to label its products with the health claim that eating oat bran lowers cholesterol. [12]The FDA approves only health claims that have research to support them.

E [13]Fortified foods have added vitamins and minerals. [14]This idea started in 1830 when a chemist discovered that adding iodine to salt prevented an enlarged thyroid gland, or goiter. [15]The newest trend in fortified foods is adding herbs. [16]Food companies have started making claims that these herbs will improve your health and even prevent disease. [17]Tea with added ginseng says it gives you "a positive energy boost." [18]Soup with echinacea claims to "fortify the immune system." [19]Are these claims facts or opinions?

F [20]Many people believe herbs improve health and prevent disease. [21]However, most herbs have never been tested to find out if this is true. [22]There are no standards for products that contain herbs. [23]Nor is there evidence to prove their claims as food additives.

G [24]Functional foods may prove to be of great benefit to people. [25]However, it is important to look for evidence of testing before believing what the product says. [26]Not all health claims may be facts.

DIRECTIONS: Circle the letter next to the correct answer or write the answer on the lines given. When asked for evidence, write the number of the sentence or the letter of the paragraph that best supports the answer.

1. According to the article, which of the following sentences is a fact?
   ___ Oat bran helps to lower cholesterol.
   ___ Tea with ginseng gives an energy boost.

   Explain the answer.

   _____

   _____

   _____

2. Which two of the following can help you decide if a health claim is fact or opinion?
   A. reading the fine print
   B. checking for FDA approval
   C. trying the food out yourself
   D. looking for testing

   Which sentence is the best evidence? ____

3. Based on the article, label the following statements as fact or opinion. (F or O)
   ___ Quaker Oats has products with an FDA label.
   ___ Herbs added to foods can improve health.
   ___ Ginseng is an herb.
   ___ Functional foods are of great benefit to people.

4. Why should you be careful about believing the claims on health foods?

   _____

   _____

   Which paragraph is the best evidence? ____

38. *Sing Down the Moon* (Excerpt)
by Scott O'Dell

A [1]"These Navahos are happy with their dogs," he said. [2]"Happy girls bring better prices than unhappy girls. [3]That I have learned and do not need to learn again."

B [4]The fourth night when the moon was overhead, I saw dim lights in the distance and soon we came to a place where white people lived. [5]There was a wide street with many houses along it and many trees in a row.

. . .

C [6]"It is dog meat," I said to Running Bird.

D [7]"Yes, it is dog and an old one," she said.

E [8]The woman started to fill two bowls with the stew. [9]By signs I told her that we had eaten and were not hungry. [10]I did not try to tell her that my people, the Navahos, never ate stew made of dog meat.

F [11]The old woman spread a blanket on the floor for Running Bird and me to sleep on. [12]Then she spread a blanket for herself and lay down in front of that door, so that we could not open it. [13]I was tired, but I did not sleep. [14]I made my black dog lie down beside me. [15]I had seen the old woman eyeing him and I was afraid that if I went to sleep she would kill him to make a stew.

G [16]Early the next morning the Spaniard with the white teeth came back. [17]He gave the old woman a silver coin, which she hid in her mouth. [18]Then he motioned me to follow him. [19]Running Bird held on to me until the Spaniard pulled us apart. [20]I did not know what to say to her. [21]I went out of the hut and the Spaniard got on his horse and I followed him, the black dog walking beside me.

H [22]As we left the hut, the old woman hobbled after us and threw a leather rope around the dog's neck and tried to drag him back.

I [23]The Spaniard wheeled his horse around. [24]"Let the dog loose," he said, "I will bring you another, a fatter one."

J [25]The old woman did as she was told and the three of us left her and went down the street.

K [26]There was no one around. [27]When we were almost at the end of the street I saw a girl sweeping the earth in front of a gate. [28]She was an Indian and had the marks of the Nez Percé on her cheeks. [29]She glanced up at me, though she did not stop her sweeping. [30]It was a quick glance, yet in it was something that chilled me. [31]As if she were saying, "Run, run, even though they kill you. [32]It is better to die here on the street."

DIRECTIONS: Circle the letter next to the correct answer or write the answer on the lines given. When asked for evidence, write the number of the sentence or the letter of the paragraph that best supports the answer.

1. Much of the story takes place:
   A. in a Spanish slave village.
   B. on the road to a white town.
   C. in a tent in a Navaho village.
   D. in a hut in a white town.

2. From paragraph A, you can infer that the Spaniard:
   A. wants to sell for a good price.
   B. sells only to white people.
   C. will sell only Indian girls.
   D. has never sold girls before.

3. The Spaniard says he has learned that Navaho girls are happy with their dogs, and that happy girls bring better prices. What later paragraph supports that he has learned this lesson?

   Paragraph _____

4. In paragraph H, the old woman tries to take the dog. This is foreshadowed in which sentence?
   A. 1
   B. 10
   C. 15
   D. 24

5. What did the old woman do to prevent the girls from escaping while she slept?

   _____

6. Number the following events in correct order.
   __ The Spaniard and girls arrive at the white people's place.
   __ The narrator sees a warning in the glance of a girl who is sweeping.
   __ The woman catches the dog.
   __ The Spaniard pays the old woman.

7. In paragraph K, you can infer that the narrator thought the Indian girl:
   A. enjoyed sweeping.
   B. wished she could escape.
   C. had been caught escaping.
   D. had grown up there.

   Which sentence is the best evidence? _____

39. Swim for Your Life
by M. A. Hockett

A [1]Amanda had always looked up to her dad, who could do just about anything. [2]Amanda didn't think she was very good at much. [3]One thing she *could* do was swim. [4]She just hoped she was good enough. [5]Their lives depended on it now!

B [6]They had been boating through the caverns when the earthquake hit. [7]As a result of the quake, a huge boulder blocked the opening of the cave, and trapped them! [8]Was there a passage through the water under the boulder? [9]She had to find out.

C [10]She held her breath and took clean, powerful strokes. [11]There was just enough light to let her see. [12]First, she'd gone deep, then the rock sloped upward and out of the water, allowing her to rise slowly to the surface.

D [13]"Yahoo!" she couldn't help yelling with the breath that remained in her lungs. [14]Under the rock was the only way out, but it wasn't too far. [15]She found a place to tie the line she had pulled from the boat. [16]It would help keep the others on course. [17]She went back to get them.

E [18]Amanda helped her brother, sister, and mother follow the line under the rock, one at a time. [19]Dad had insisted on staying until last.

F [20]"Okay, Dad, everyone else is safe. [21]Let's go!" she said eagerly.

G [22]"I-I can't," he said. [23]"I don't know how to swim." [24]"Yes, you c—" Amanda started to dispute what he said then stopped. [25]She realized that she'd never seen her father swim.

H [26]"I'll drown if I try. [27]Send help for me later," he said. [28]"Go on!"

I [29]"No, just take a big breath and dive. [30]I'll pull you under the rock. [31]It isn't far—" [32]They both heard rumbling as new boulders angrily rushed at them from behind. [33]"Too late to argue!" Amanda yelled as she yanked her father under the water.

J [34]As she pulled him under the big rock, the line loosened. [35]The boulders must have smashed the boat. [36]Turning her head, Amanda saw the terror on her father's face just as he grabbed at her neck. [37]She ducked under his hands, then forced them around the line. [38]She surged ahead and towed him. [39]She surfaced and pulled him to shallow water. [40]Dad sputtered and choked, but he was all right.

K [41]"Amanda, you're our hero!" Mom cried. [42]The whole family hugged her. [43]They were tired and wet but happy to be out in the sunshine. [44]Amanda felt warm inside and out as they hiked to the road.

DIRECTIONS: Circle the letter next to the correct answer or write the answer on the lines given. When asked for evidence, write the number of the sentence or the letter of the paragraph that best supports the answer.

1. Which of the following best describes the theme of the story?
   A. All fathers should swim better than their children.
   B. Sometimes we can help those we look up to.
   C. Sometimes we have to sacrifice to do what is right.
   D. Boating near caverns is too dangerous.

2. In sentence 24, which choice could be used in place of *dispute*?
   A. agree with
   B. argue against
   C. repeat
   D. explain

3. What caused the cave opening to be blocked?

   _____

   Which two sentences are the best evidence?____, ____

   Which signal words are a clue?

   _____

4. What do you think would have happened if Amanda did what Dad told her to in sentence 27?

   _____

   _____

   Which sentence is the best evidence? ____

5. Paragraph I uses the words *boulders angrily rushed*. This is an example of:
   A. idiom.
   B. metaphor.
   C. simile.
   D. personification.

6. Describe the conflict between the family and the boulder.

   _____

   _____

   _____

7. How does Amanda resolve the conflict with her dad? She:
   A. continues to argue with him.
   B. convinces him to try swimming.
   C. grabs him and pulls him under.
   D. agrees to go on without him.

   Which sentence is the best evidence? ____

8. How does the mood of the story change between paragraphs J and K?

   _____

   _____

   _____

40. The Last Will
by Cheryl Block

A ¹The family would be at Sarah's office soon for the reading of Samuel's will. ²Sarah was not looking forward to it. ³She had been Samuel Goode's lawyer for many years. ⁴He had been such a kind, gentle man. ⁵But his sister Agnes was as sour as a pickle and didn't get along with anyone, not even her own sons. ⁶Mr. Goode took care of Agnes and her sons after her husband died. ⁷Although he was very generous, Agnes was always complaining about money. ⁸Sarah knew Agnes would be upset when the will was read. ⁹Agnes expected her brother to leave his fortune to her.

B ¹⁰Agnes was bringing her two grown sons and stern Mrs. Frump, the housekeeper. ¹¹Sarah felt they all had taken advantage of Mr. Goode's kind nature. ¹²And they all wanted his money, especially Agnes.

C ¹³Samuel, however, had also supported education all his life. ¹⁴Sarah could still see his face beaming as he handed her a check for the first annual Goode Grammar Award. ¹⁵"My dream has come true, Sarah." ¹⁶Good grammar had been very important to Samuel; his own grammar was always perfect. ¹⁷His will set up a fund to continue the award.

D ¹⁸Sarah jumped as the buzzer rang. ¹⁹The secretary led the family into the office. ²⁰Before Sarah could speak, Agnes handed her a paper. ²¹"Samuel wrote a new will a few days before he died. ²²We all signed it. ²³This new will replaces the one you have." ²⁴Agnes smiled smugly.

E ²⁵"Well, let me look it over," Sarah replied, trying to keep calm. ²⁶The handwritten will looked real. ²⁷The writing was hard to read, but it looked like his, and she recognized Samuel's unique signature.

F ²⁸"You can see Samuel signed it," Agnes pointed at the will.

G ²⁹"Yes, I see that," Sarah replied. ³⁰But had he written it, she wondered. ³¹"I guess we should read *this* will, then." ³²Sarah's eyes lit up as soon as she read the first sentence.

³³I, Samuel Goode, being of sound mind, hereby declare that this here is my last will and testament. ³⁴Everything I own I gives to my beloved sister and nephews.

H ³⁵"Well," Sarah paused, looking at each of them. ³⁶"You all agree that you saw Samuel *write* and sign this new will?"

I ³⁷They all nodded.

J ³⁸"Well, you won't get away with it! ³⁹This will is a fake, and I can prove it!" Sarah declared.

DIRECTIONS: Circle the letter next to the correct answer or write the answer on the lines given. When asked for evidence, write the number of the sentence or the letter of the paragraph that best supports the answer.

1. Which of the following is the best theme for the story?
   A. Blood is thicker than water.
   B. Lawyers always win.
   C. Cheaters never win.
   D. Good grammar is important.

2. Paragraph A uses a simile to describe which character?
   A. Samuel
   B. Sarah
   C. Agnes
   D. Mr. Goode

   Write the simile used.

   _____

3. Sarah has a flashback about:
   A. Agnes and her sons.
   B. Samuel's new will.
   C. the Grammar Award.
   D. Mrs. Frump.

   Which two sentences are the best evidence? ____, ____

4. The main conflict in the story was between:
   A. Sarah and Samuel.
   B. Samuel and his sister.
   C. Sarah and Agnes.
   D. Agnes and her sons.

5. In the story, Sarah felt Agnes was:
   A. easily upset.
   B. greedy.
   C. very pushy.
   D. friendly.

   Which two sentences are the best evidence? ____, ____

6. In sentence 32, what does the idiom "eyes lit up" mean? Sarah's eyes:
   A. glowed like a lamp.
   B. got wider with interest.
   C. caught fire.
   D. closed in boredom.

7. How did Sarah conclude the will was a fake?
   A. It contained no errors.
   B. Samuel's signature was different.
   C. It contained grammar errors.
   D. Samuel didn't love his sister.

   Which two sentences are the best evidence? ____, ____

41. The Working Child
by Christine Broz

A [1]If you were a child living in New England one hundred years ago, you might have worked twelve hours a day in a textile mill, a factory that made cloth. [2]Many children of that time spent their entire childhood in the unhealthy and dangerous mills. [3]Their families needed the income from all family members in order to have enough to live. [4]There was hardly time for school or even just playing like a child.

B [5]Working in a textile mill was not healthy. [6]Often there was not enough fresh air. [7]The windows were kept closed to prevent breezes or humidity from affecting the weaving machines. [8]There was lots of cotton dust from the machines floating about in the air, so the workers sometimes had trouble breathing. [9]The mills were cold in the winter and hot and humid in the summer. [10]The children stood on their feet all day long. [11]They didn't get enough exercise or the chance to play. [12]Often they were tired from getting up before dawn and working until dark.

C [13]Working around fast-moving machines was dangerous. [14]It was the job of children to replace empty bobbins. [15]The bobbins were wooden dowels wound with the thread used to weave the cloth. [16]The children also had to quickly repair broken threads on the machines. [17]Some children were so small they had to climb up onto the machines to do the work. [18]This put them at greater risk for getting hurt. [19]Many injuries resulted when the hands, feet, hair, or clothing of workers got caught in the machinery.

D [20]Most children of mill workers did not have the chance to go to school. [21]They worked alongside the adults six days a week for twelve hours a day. [22]On their day off, they might go to Sunday school, where they learned some writing and arithmetic. [23]Their lack of education meant they would not become skilled enough to do anything but work in a factory when they grew up.

E [24]It was a tough life for children. [25]Today, there are laws that require children to go to school and laws that prevent children from working. [26]The government hopes that children will grow up healthy, educated and able to support themselves as adults.

DIRECTIONS: Circle the letter next to the correct answer or write the answer on the lines given. When asked for evidence, write the number of the sentence or the letter of the paragraph that best supports the answer.

1. What is the main idea of the article?
    A. Children and adults worked in the textile mills.
    B. Children liked working in the mills.
    C. Children made a lot of money working in the mills.
    D. Children once worked long hours in dangerous mills.

2. In sentence 1, the word *textile* means:
    A. fabric.
    B. factory.
    C. food.
    D. bobbin.

    Which word is a context clue?

    _____

3. Why did children work in textile mills?

    _____

    _____

    Which sentence is the best evidence? _____

4. Children working in the mills had breathing problems because:
    A. they breathed in cotton dust.
    B. they breathed in cold air.
    C. they didn't get any exercise.
    D. they couldn't go to the doctor.

    Which sentence gives the best evidence? _____

    Which word is a signal? _____

5. Which one of the following sentences is an opinion?
    A. Sentence 20
    B. Sentence 21
    C. Sentence 24
    D. Sentence 25

    Which word in the sentence gives a clue? _____

6. Give one example of why working in a textile mill was unhealthy.

    _____

    _____

7. Based on the article, you could conclude that:
    A. children liked working with their parents.
    B. adults didn't want children in the mills.
    C. children preferred school to work.
    D. adults were not paid enough to support a family.

42. *Owls in the Family* (Excerpt)
by Farley Mowat

A [1]Mother and Dad and I were having dinner. [2]The dining room windows were open because it had been such a hot day. [3]All of a sudden there was a great *swooooosh* of wings—and there, on the window sill, sat Wol. [4]Before any of us had time to move, he gave a leap and landed on the floor beside my chair. [5]And he hadn't come empty-handed. [6]Clutched in his talons was an enormous skunk. [7]The skunk was dead, but that didn't help matters much because, before he died, he had managed to soak himself and Wol with his own special brand of perfume.

B [8]"Hoo-hoohoohoo-HOO!" Wol said proudly.

C [9]Which probably meant: "Mind if I join you? [10]I've brought my supper with me."

D [11]Nobody stopped to answer. [12]We three people were already stampeding through the door of the dining room, coughing and choking. [13]Wol had to eat his dinner by himself.

E [14]It was two weeks before we could use the dining room again, and when Mother sent the rug and drapes to the cleaners, the man who owned the shop phoned her right back and wanted to know if she was trying to ruin him.

F [15]Wol didn't smell so sweet either, but he couldn't understand why he was so unpopular all of a sudden. [16]His feelings must have been hurt by the way everybody kept trying to avoid him. [17]After two or three days, when even I wouldn't go near him, or let him come near me, he became very unhappy. [18]Then an idea must have come into his funny head. [19]He must have decided we were mad at him because he hadn't shared his skunk with us! [20]So one day he went down to the riverbank and caught a second skunk, and brought it home for us.

G [21]By this time he was so soaked in skunk oil that you could smell him a block away. [22]Some of our neighbors complained about it, and so finally my father had to give Wol a bath in about a gallon of tomato juice. [23]Tomato juice is the only thing that will wash away the smell of skunk.

H [24]Poor Wol! [25]By the time Dad was through with him he looked like a rag mop that had been dipped in ketchup. [26]But he got the idea, and he never again brought his skunks home to us.

DIRECTIONS: Circle the letter next to the correct answer or write the answer on the lines given. When asked for evidence, write the number of the sentence or the letter of the paragraph that best supports the answer.

1. Paragraph A suggests that the family was:
   A. pleased by Wol's arrival.
   B. expecting Wol to arrive.
   C. surprised by Wol's arrival.
   D. unaware of Wol's arrival.

   Which two sentences are the best evidence? _____, _____

2. The family was unable to use the dining room for two weeks because:
   A. Wol's supper was still there.
   B. the room still smelled of skunk.
   C. it was too hot to eat in there.
   D. Mother wanted to wait for the rug and drapes.

3. In sentence 3, why does the author use *swooooosh* to describe Wol's arrival?

   _____

   _____

4. Based on his behavior, you can conclude that Wol:
   A. did not like getting dirty.
   B. wanted to please the family.
   C. was afraid of people.
   D. did not like to share.

   Which two sentences are the best evidence? _____, _____

5. In paragraph F, the narrator gives Wol's point of view in human terms. Give one example.

   _____

   _____

6a. What was the main problem in the story?

   _____

   _____

b. How did the family resolve the problem?

   _____

7. Write the simile used in paragraph H.

   _____

   _____

8. Which is the most likely reason that Wol never brought a skunk home again?
   A. He didn't want the neighbors to get mad at him.
   B. He decided to bring home squirrels instead.
   C. He didn't want another tomato juice bath.
   D. He didn't want to mess up the house.

   Which sentence is the best evidence? _____

43. Tiger Woods: Golfing Legend
by Cheryl Block

A [1]Tiger Woods rose to stardom in the sport of golf at an early age. [2]Eldrick "Tiger" Woods started swinging a golf club at age two. [3]By age twenty-one, he was ranked number one in the golfing world.

B [4]Tiger has made golfing history. [5]At age eighteen, he was the youngest player ever to win the U.S. Amateur golf tournament. [6]He is the only player to win this title three straight times. [7]Tiger became a professional golfer in 1996. [8]He went on to become the youngest winner of the Masters Golf Tournament when he was twenty-one. [9]The Masters, which was started in 1934, is one of four major championships in golf. [10]Tiger has won almost every major golf event at least once and the Masters three times to date.

C [11]Tiger gives his dad, who passed away in 2006, a lot of credit for his success. [12]"My father always instilled in me there are only two things in life that you ought to do. [13]You gotta care and you gotta share."

D [14]Tiger has used his success to encourage other young people. [15]Tiger and his father started the Tiger Woods Foundation in 1996. [16]Its mission is "to empower young people to reach their highest potential." [17]The Foundation has contributed to youth programs throughout 30 states. [18]Tiger gives not only his money but also his time. [19]The Foundation has sponsored clinics that give kids a chance to meet their hero while raising funds for local groups. [20]Through his foundation, Tiger wants to "help teach kids that if they dream big enough, miracles can happen." [21]Jacci Woods of the Young Minority Golf Association in Detroit says, "He's a real inspiration for the kids."

E [22]Tiger's ethnic background has also made him a pioneer in golf. [23]Tiger is the first Black or Asian golfer to become a world champion. [24]His dad was African-American and his mother is Asian. [25]However, as Tiger himself states, "I am an American... and proud of it!"

DIRECTIONS: Circle the letter next to the correct answer or write the answer on the lines given. When asked for evidence, write the number of the sentence or the letter of the paragraph that best supports the answer.

1. Which sentence from the passage is an opinion?
   A. Tiger has made golfing history.
   B. He is the only player to win the title three times.
   C. Tiger has used his success to encourage other young people.
   D. "He's a real inspiration for the kids."

2. From paragraphs C and D, you can infer that Tiger and his dad
   A. were good friends.
   B. shared a desire to help others.
   C. liked to work together.
   D. had nothing in common.

   Which three sentences are the best evidence? _____, _____, _____

3. Based on the article, Tiger's point of view is that:
   A. it is important to encourage kids.
   B. it is best to start sports when you are young.
   C. you should be the best person you can.
   D. winning is everything.

   Which sentence is the best evidence? _____

4. In sentence 22, the word *ethnic* could be replaced with:
   A. racial.
   B. athletic.
   C. golfing.
   D. educational.

   Which sentence is the best evidence? _____

5. Tiger made golfing history by
   A. starting to play at age two.
   B. being the youngest winner of major golf events.
   C. becoming a professional golfer.
   D. being ranked number one in golf.

   Which two sentences are the best evidence? _____, _____

6. What is the main idea of paragraph D?
   A. Tiger's Foundation encourages young people.
   B. Tiger's dad was his role model.
   C. Tiger is a hero.
   D. Tiger started the Tiger Woods Foundation.

44. Geocaching
by Christine Broz

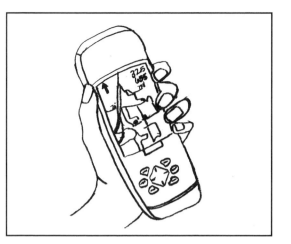

A ¹There is a new kind of treasure hunt called geocaching (pronounced geo cashing). ²The goal of this adventure game is to find a cache, a container of hidden goods.

B ³A cache is put together and hidden by one person. ⁴It is usually held in a waterproof container. ⁵It contains a logbook with information written about the contents of the cache and the area where it is hidden. ⁶The cache may contain common, unusual, or valuable items. ⁷It may include such things as CDs, software, jewelry, money, antiques, maps, stamps, photos, or other trinkets.

C ⁸A player uses a high tech gadget called a GPS (Global Positioning System) receiver to find the cache. ⁹The GPS was originally developed by the military as a navigation tool. ¹⁰Now anyone can buy one. ¹¹It is about the size of a cell phone and uses data from satellites that are 12,000 miles up in space. ¹²The GPS receiver can tell the user his or her exact location on Earth—anywhere in the 197 million square miles of land and sea. ¹³It helps a player get to within 10 feet of the hidden treasure.

D ¹⁴Learning where the cache is hidden is the easy part. ¹⁵Actually finding the treasure is the challenge. ¹⁶The waypoint of a cache is posted on a computer website by the person who hid it. ¹⁷The waypoint tells the longitude and latitude coordinates of the cache. ¹⁸The cache may be located in a city park or off a wilderness trail.

E ¹⁹The player enters the waypoint into the GPS unit. ²⁰Then the player uses an electronic map on the GPS or a paper map to determine the general area of the waypoint and the best starting point. ²¹When the player gets to the starting point, he or she enters this location into the GPS. ²²The GPS tracks the player's movements in relation to the waypoint. ²³It shows if he or she is getting closer. ²⁴If a player gets lost, the GPS receiver is helpful for backtracking to the starting point. ²⁵Once the player gets to the waypoint, he or she must rely on eyesight to pinpoint the cache, which can be hidden behind or under something.

F ²⁶The basic rules of the game are that the player takes something from the cache, leaves something, and writes about the adventure in the log book. ²⁷For many players, the fun and adventure of locating the "treasure" is as important as the prize.

DIRECTIONS: Circle the letter next to the correct answer or write the answer on the lines given. When asked for evidence, write the number of the sentence or the letter of the paragraph that best supports the answer.

1. What does the word *cache* mean?
   A. money
   B. hidden supply
   C. adventure game
   D. secret location

   Which sentence is the best evidence? ____

2. Label the following sentences F for fact or O for opinion.
   __ Sentence 14
   __ Sentence 15
   __ Sentence 16
   __ Sentence 17

3. What is the main idea of the article?
   A. Geocaching uses modern technology to find treasure.
   B. GPS receivers make finding caches fun.
   C. Finding a cache is not as fun as the adventure.
   D. GPS receivers are very powerful navigation tools.

4. Is sentence 11 a topic sentence or a supporting detail?

   _____

5. Which sentence in paragraph C contains the main idea of the paragraph?
   A. 8   C. 12
   B. 10   D. 13

6. Sentence 24 says the GPS receiver can help someone who is lost. This conclusion is based on

   _____

   _____

7. In which situation would you predict that a GPS receiver would be helpful?
   A. navigating the Internet
   B. locating meteors in space
   C. scuba diving to sunken ships
   D. finding a missing dog

8. Since GPS receivers transfer data over a great distance you could infer that they:
   A. cost a lot of money.
   B. are hard to learn to use.
   C. are powerful navigation tools.
   D. know the exact location of a cache.

Fiction Posttest:
"For the Love of a Man" from *The Call of the Wild* (Excerpt)
by Jack London

A [1]At a particularly bad spot, where a ledge of barely submerged rocks jutted out into the river, Hans cast off the rope, and, while Thornton poled the boat out into the stream, ran down the bank with the end in his hand to snub* the boat when it had cleared the ledge. [2]This it did, and was flying downstream in a current as swift as a mill-race, when Hans checked (stopped) it with the rope and checked too suddenly. [3]The boat flirted over and snubbed in to the bank bottom up, while Thornton, flung sheer out of it, was carried downstream toward the worst part of the rapids, a stretch of wild water in which no swimmer could live.

B [4]Buck had sprung in an instant; and at the end of three hundred yards, amid a mad swirl of water, he overhauled Thornton. [5]When he felt him grasp his tail, Buck headed for the bank, swimming with all his splendid strength. [6]But the progress shoreward was slow; the progress downstream amazingly rapid. [7]From below came the fatal roaring where the wild current went wilder and was rent in shreds and spray by the rocks which thrust through like the teeth of an enormous comb. [8]The suck of the water as it took the beginning of the last steep pitch was frightful, and Thornton knew that the shore was impossible. [9]He scraped furiously over a rock, bruised across a second, and struck a third with crushing force. [10]He clutched its slippery top with both hands, releasing Buck, and above the roar of the churning water shouted: "Go, Buck! Go!"

C [11]Buck could not hold his own, and swept on downstream, struggling desperately, but unable to win back.

[12]When he heard Thornton's command repeated, he partly reared out of the water, throwing his head high, as though a last look, then turned obediently toward the bank. [13]He swam powerfully, and was dragged ashore by Pete and Hans at the very point where swimming ceased to be possible and destruction began.

D [14]They knew that the time a man could cling to a slippery rock in the face of that driving current was a matter of minutes, and they ran as fast as they could up the bank to a point far above where Thornton was hanging on. [15]They attached the line with which they had been snubbing the boat to Buck's neck and shoulders, being careful that it should neither strangle him nor impede his swimming, and launched him into the stream. [16]He struck out boldly, but not straight enough into the stream. [17]He discovered the mistake too late, when Thornton was abreast of him and a bare half-dozen strokes away while he was being carried helplessly past.

E [18]Hans promptly snubbed with the rope, as though Buck were a boat. [19]The rope thus tightening on him in the sweep of the current, he was jerked under the surface, and under the surface he remained till his body struck against the bank and he was hauled out. [20]He was half drowned, and Hans and Pete threw themselves upon him, pounding the breath into him and the water out of him. [21]He staggered to his feet and fell down. [22]The faint sound of Thornton's voice came to them, and though they could not make out the words of it, they knew that he was in his extremity. [23]His master's voice acted on Buck like an electric shock. [24]He sprang to his feet and ran up the bank ahead of the men to the point of his previous departure.

*snub: to secure a boat by wrapping the line around a post

DIRECTIONS: Circle the letter next to the correct answer or write the answer on the lines given. When asked for evidence, write the number of the sentence or the letter of the paragraph that best supports the answer.

1. Which of the following is the best theme for the passage?
   A. Only the fittest survive in the wilderness.
   B. Whitewater is dangerous.
   C. An animal's love can be strong.
   D. All animals love people.

2. The boat turns over because
   A. Hans let go of the rope.
   B. Thornton dropped the pole.
   C. Hans stopped the boat too quickly.
   D. the boat hit the submerged rocks.

   Which sentence is the best evidence? _____

3. Which sentence in paragraph B best supports the inference that Buck is probably a dog?

   Sentence _____

4. What does the word *rent* mean in sentence 7?
   A. leased
   B. torn
   C. bent
   D. spread

   Which words in the sentence are the best context clues?

   _____

5. Write the simile used to describe the rocks in paragraph B.

   _____

6. The main conflict in the story is between:
   A. Buck and Thornton.
   B. Pete and Hans.
   C. Buck and the river.
   D. Hans and Thornton.

7. Which best describes Buck's character in the story?
   A. frightened
   B. determined
   C. poorly trained
   D. angry

   Explain your answer.

   _____

   _____

   _____

8. What does the word *impede* in sentence 15 mean?
   A. reverse
   B. support
   C. speed
   D. obstruct

9. In sentence 17, Buck concludes he should have:
   A. gone straight.
   B. gone more slowly.
   C. swum faster.
   D. stayed on shore.

   Which sentence is the best evidence? ____

10. What kind of figurative language is used in sentence 23?
    A. personification
    B. idiom
    C. simile
    D. metaphor

11. At what point does the story reach a crisis?
    A. Thornton is thrown into the river.
    B. Buck is carried past Thornton on his second try.
    C. Thornton lets go of Buck's tail.
    D. Thornton is clinging to a rock.

    Which two sentences are the best evidence? ____, ____

12. Predict what Buck will do next.

    _____

    _____

    _____

Nonfiction Posttest:
The *Spirit of Freedom*
by Cheryl Block

A [1]Steve Fossett loved a good challenge. [2]He holds seven official world speed records in sailing. [3]He swam the English Channel and competed in Alaska's Iditarod Dogsled Race. [4]On July 4, 2002, Steve Fossett landed his balloon in the Australian Outback, ending his record-breaking trip around the world in less than 15 days. [5]Fossett was the first person to ever finish a solo flight around the world in a hot-air balloon.

B [6]Fossett made five previous tries before setting the record, each one with its own set of dangers. [7]During one 1998 trip, the balloon ruptured during a thunderstorm. [8]Falling at 3500 feet per minute, he was able to cut away some of the fuel tanks and slow his fall. [9]Fossett dropped into the Coral Sea below. [10]At first, he was knocked unconscious by the impact, but he managed to climb out of the capsule and into a life raft. [11]He was rescued 23 hours later. [12]In his 2001 trip, severe weather again caused him to end his attempt. [13]Even his successful trip had its dangers when a hose on one of the propane burners caught fire just hours before he landed.

C [14]Fossett told reporters that he had one of his worst landings that time. [15]He had to wait an extra day till gusty winds died down somewhat.

[16]The system for deflating the balloon didn't work. [17]Strong winds dragged the balloon along for nearly three miles before he could detach the capsule.

D [18]Living in a hot-air balloon for two weeks wasn't easy either. [19]Fossett's balloon has a closed capsule that is about the size of a closet and holds a bunk with a sleeping bag. [20]Fossett was able to sleep only about four hours a day, usually 45 minutes at a time. [21]He lived on army-type rations and water. [22]The capsule of the balloon is not pressurized like an airplane cabin, so Fossett had to breathe through an oxygen mask during his flight. [23]The capsule does have a heating system because the temperatures outside the balloon can drop well below zero.

E [24]Fossett began this trip in Australia on June 18, 2002. [25]It took him exactly 13 days, 12 hours, 16 minutes and 13 seconds to circle the Southern Hemisphere of Earth. [26]He used a GPS* device to navigate and stay on course.

F [27]After six tries, Fossett had succeeded in his latest challenge. [28]His hot-air balloon, the *Spirit of Freedom*, was given to the Smithsonian Institute's National Air and Space Museum. [29]It will hang right next to the airplane of another great world adventurer, Charles Lindbergh, the first man to fly solo across the Atlantic Ocean.

*GPS: Global Positioning System

DIRECTIONS: Circle the letter next to the correct answer or write the answer on the lines given. When asked for evidence, write the number of the sentence or the letter of the paragraph that best supports the answer.

1. What is the main idea of the article?
   A. Steve Fossett set many different world records.
   B. Steve Fossett overcame danger to make the first solo balloon flight around Earth.
   C. Steve Fossett tried six times to circle the globe in his hot-air balloon.
   D. Steve Fossett spent two weeks living in a balloon.

2. Fossett was involved in several endurance sports. Give one example.

   _____

3. What is the main idea of paragraph B?
   A. Severe weather affected every flight.
   B. Each attempt was dangerous.
   C. Balloon flying requires skill.
   D. Fossett had to rely on others to save him.

   Which sentence is the best evidence? _____

4. From paragraph C, you can infer that wind during a landing:
   A. has no effect.
   B. provides a softer landing.
   C. can keep the balloon from deflating.
   D. may drag the balloon.

   Which sentence is the best evidence? _____

5. Which of the following is a supporting detail of paragraph D?
   A. The capsule's interior was small.
   B. He wore an oxygen mask only at night.
   C. The capsule was not heated.
   D. He slept forty-five minutes a day.

   Which sentence is the best evidence? _____

6. Since the cabin was not pressurized, Fossett:
   A. could sleep only a short time.
   B. had to wear an oxygen mask.
   C. had to fly at a lower altitude.
   D. had to keep the cabin heated.

   Which sentence is the best evidence? _____

7. Label the following statements as fact or opinion (F/O).

___ Temperatures dropped below zero outside the capsule.

___ Fossett was the world's greatest adventurer.

8. Based on his history, you could have probably predicted that Fossett:

   A. was ready to retire.

   B. would seek a new adventure.

   C. preferred sailing to ballooning.

   D. would not fly again.

ANSWER KEY

The answer key provides the following information: a copy of the student passage with superscripted numbers, questions with the reading skill in parentheses, the correct answer given in bolded text, the numbers or letters of the evidence sentences or paragraphs, and an explanation of the answer (when necessary). Reading levels are given for each story.

Although we give a recommended answer choice for each question, teachers should discuss any different responses with students to clarify their reasoning. If the teacher feels a student has made a good case for a response, based on the evidence in the passage, the teacher may want to accept the student's answer, also.

For the short answer questions, students do not have to follow the suggested wording exactly as long as they include the key information needed to answer the question. The literature and fiction stories, in particular, are open to greater interpretation than the nonfiction as to author meaning. The primary focus of this program is to get students to think about what they read and to improve their understanding of the material. You may find your students involved in a lively debate as to which is the best answer to a question. By all means, encourage this!

How to Be a Reading Detective (p. 1)

1. You can conclude that if the new growth is gone, the plants
   A. will take longer to grow.
   B. will not grow back.
   C. will not be affected.
   D. will grow elsewhere.

   Two best evidence sentences: **6, 7**

   Explain how the evidence supports your answer.

   If the new shoots are gone, the grass is not able to grow again.

Explanation: Sentence 6 states that native animals leave the new shoots so they will sprout again. Sentence 7 states that cattle are destroying the grasslands because they eat all of the grass.

PRETESTS

Fiction Pretest: The Runaway (p. 2)
Reading Level: 4.2

1. What is the theme of the story?
   A. A dog is a man's best friend.
   B. Dogs can adapt to anything.
   C. You can learn from your mistakes.
   D. Sometimes things get worse before they get better.

   Explanation: D is the best choice because the dog went through difficult times before she found a home. B is contradicted by paragraph B. There is no evidence for the other choices.

2. In sentence 5, what does the word *reluctant* mean?
   A. unable
   B. unwilling
   C. unlucky
   D. unhappy

   Which words are a context clue?

   had talked (into)

   Explanation: If you talk someone into something, it means they are not willing to do it at first.

3. The story takes place in (setting)
   A. a city.
   B. a park.
   C. the country.
   D. the wilderness.

   Best evidence sentence: **13**

   Explanation: Sentence 13 refers to streets and neighborhood.

4. What can you infer the dog did because she was lonely and scared in paragraph B?

She started to chew on the rug and furniture.

Best evidence sentence: **9**

Explanation: Sentence 7 states the dog was scared and lonely. Sentence 9 says she started chewing on the rug and furniture.

5. What caused the dog to put her tail between her legs when she was walking the streets?

fear

What words in sentence 18 are a clue?

as a result of

6. Put the following events in order.
   3 Dog is taken to animal shelter.
   5 Dog is adopted by family.
   2 Dog is unhappy and escapes.
   1 Dog's owner goes away and leaves her with a friend.
   4 Dog is unhappy and can't escape.

7. The story reaches a crisis when the dog (plot)
   A. loses her owner.
   B. goes to the friend's house.
   C. is lost in the neighborhood.
   D. is taken to the shelter.

Two best evidence sentences: **25, 26**

Explanation: D is the best choice because the story has reached a point where the dog can no longer control events. Something must happen to resolve the dog's situation. She will either get a home or be put to sleep. The other choices are key events, but each is quickly resolved by the next event.

8. Which sentence in paragraph E contains a simile?

Sentence **31**

Write the simile.

(her coat was) **as rich and brown as chocolate**

9. From whose point of view is the story told?
   A. the friend's
   B. the dog's
   C. Tim's
   D. the new owner's

Explanation: The events are seen through the dog's eyes. You are even told what the dog is thinking.

10. Which sentence in paragraph C foreshadows the dog ending up in the shelter?

Sentence **17**

Explanation: The dog noticed the white truck with bars in the neighborhood. It was the same truck that later took her to the pound.

11. Do you think the dog will try to escape from her new home? Explain your answer.

No. The dog seems content in the new home.

Best evidence sentence: **32**

She thinks "*This* is better than anything."

Nonfiction Pretest: Teen Sleep (p. 5)
Reading level: 5.1

1. What is the main idea of the article?
   A. Children and teens have different sleep needs.
   B. Teens have busy schedules.
   C. Teens need to get more sleep.
   D. Some schools adjust their schedules for teens.

Explanation: C is the best choice because the article explains why teens are sleep deprived and gives reasons why they need more sleep. The other choices are supporting details.

2. What does the word *insufficient* mean in sentence 9?
   A. adequate
   B. not enough
   C. too great
   D. interrupted

   Which other sentence gives a context clue? **10**

   Explanation: Since teens need 9–10 hours of sleep, the words *less than* in sentence 10 reinforce that an insufficient amount is not enough sleep.

3. In sentence 13, what does the phrase *brains can be "foggy"* mean? (idiom)

   They are not thinking clearly.

   Sentence 12 also states that they are *not alert* because they are sleepy.

4. The topic sentence of paragraph B is sentence **9.**

   The paragraph explains why teens are sleep deprived.

5. Why do some schools have later start times? (reading for detail, cause/effect)

   so teens get more time in the morning to sleep

   Best evidence sentence: **19**

6. From paragraph C, you could infer that
   A. **people cannot think or act as well when they are tired.**
   B. teens prefer afterschool activities or jobs to school.
   C. schools starting later will solve teens' problems.

D. people should get at least ten hours of sleep at night.

Explanation: Lack of sleep can affect teens' learning and lead to bad choices and behavioral problems.

7. Paragraph D supports the conclusion that
   A. **some schools are attempting to meet students' needs.**
   B. schools are making students improve their sleep habits.
   C. school hours are getting longer.
   D. school schedules don't need change.

Explanation: The paragraph gives examples of schools that have made schedule changes to meet teens' needs.

8. Label the following statements with F for fact or O for opinion.
   F Being sleep deprived has negative effects on teens.
   F Teens need nine to ten hours of sleep each night.
   O The adolescent years are tough.

Explanation: The first two statements can be proven. In the third, the word *tough* is a subjective term that would be difficult to measure.

9. List one of the negative effects of being sleep deprived.

   Accept any one of the following:
   not alert in school (12)**; irritable or depressed** (14)**; behavioral problems** (15)**; fall asleep driving** (17)

UNIT 1 MAIN IDEA (p. 7)

Lesson Answers

1. Topic sentence in paragraph C. **11**
2. Topic sentence in D. **3**

Main Idea Practice Activity (p. 10)

1. What is the main idea of the story?
   A. **The skeleton is the framework that supports and protects the body.**

2. Which of the following is the main idea of paragraph B?
   C. **The skeleton holds the muscles.**

3. Which of the following sentences is NOT a supporting detail of paragraph B?
   D. **Muscles are part of the skeleton.**

4. How does paragraph C support the main idea of the story?

   It describes *how* the skeleton protects the body.

1. Pass the Salt (p. 12)
Reading Level: 4.8

1. Which of the following is the main idea of the story?
   A. Salt was not always easy to find.
   B. Salt was used as money to trade goods and services.
   C. **Salt has been valuable to man throughout history.**
   D. Salt makes you thirsty.

   Explanation: C is the best choice. The article explains why and how salt has been valuable. A and B are supporting details. There is no evidence of D.

2. What is the main idea of paragraph B?

   The human body needs salt to survive.

   Sentence 5 is the topic sentence.

3. What is the main idea of paragraph C?
   A. Salt used to be scarce.
   B. People built villages near salt.
   C. **People found salt in nature.**

D. Salt is found in fish and animal meat.

Two best evidence sentences: **10, 11**

Explanation: Salt was found near the ocean and in animal meat.

4. Sentence 17 supports the main idea of paragraph D that (main idea)
   A. salt made food taste better.
   B. **salt preserved food for storage.**
   C. salt could be preserved.
   D. salt made food more valuable.

5. How does paragraph E best support the idea that salt was very valuable to people in the past? It tells (supporting details)
   A. where salt is found.
   B. that salt is found in the Sahara Desert.
   C. where the word salary comes from.
   D. **how salt was used as money.**

6. Which sentence is the topic sentence in paragraph F?

   Sentence **25**

2. Day of Infamy (p. 14)
Reading Level: 3.8

1. About what time of day did the author probably write in her journal on Saturday? (sequence)
   A. 8:00 AM
   B. noon
   C. midafternoon
   D. **midnight**

   Best evidence sentence: **10**

   Explanation: Ginger uses present tense when she writes "We got home about ten of twelve and I'm very sleepy."

2. Which is the main idea of paragraph B?
   A. **BOMBED!**

B. Pearl Harbor in flames!
C. Unknown attacker so far!
D. 8:00 in the morning.

Explanation: How does sentence 15 support the main idea? **It shows the result of the bombing.**

3. Sentence 21 supports the main idea of paragraph C that (main idea)
    A. the weather was too hot.
    B. they had to leave the post.
    C. the PX and barracks are on fire.
    D. school is being discontinued.

Topic sentence: **19**

Explanation: The paragraph explains why they had to leave the post and where they went.

4. Which sentence in paragraph C supports the idea that the writer is a high school senior? (supporting detail)

Sentence **29**

Explanation: The words *school* and *there goes my graduation* imply that she was graduating from school.

5. How many were killed when the barracks were hit? (reading for detail)

350

Sentence 30 states that 350 were killed.

6. Which sentences support the idea that Saturday was a day much like any other Saturday? (supporting details)
    A. 3, 4, 6
    B. 12, 13, 14
    C. 7, 8, 9
    D. 9, 10, 11

Explanation: A is correct because activities like reading and listening to the radio are more likely regular weekend events. B is incorrect because a bombing attack is unusual. C and D are incorrect because

attending a play and getting home late from a play are probably not regular weekend events.

3. A Breed Apart (p. 16)
Reading level: 5.3

1. What is the main idea of the article?
    A. Rescue dogs risk their lives to save others.
    B. Dogs must have certain traits to be a good search and rescue dog.
    C. Dogs are carefully trained to find people.
    D. Dogs are chosen and trained for many different types of rescue.

Explanation: The article focuses on how dogs are selected and trained to be search and rescue dogs.

2. What is the main idea of paragraph B?
    A. Dogs can smell anything.
    B. Dogs can be trained to identify specific scents.
    C. Rescue dogs save firefighters time.
    D. Rescue dogs can identify a person's scent.

Explanation: Sentence 7 is the topic sentence and supports B. C and D are supporting details. There is no evidence for A.

3. In paragraph C, what are the three traits that a rescue dog needs? (reading for detail)

    1. **high energy**

    2. **fearlessness**

    3. **strong prey drive**
        (or instinct to hunt)

4. Which sentence is the topic sentence of paragraph D?

Sentence **19**

5. Which two sentences support the idea that a dog has been trained for rescue? (supporting details)
   A. It refuses to eat or drink.
   B. It can recognize a specific person's smell.
   C. It isn't afraid of people.
   D. It can walk safely over debris.

Two best evidence paragraphs: **B, D**

Explanation: A dog must be trained to recognize a certain scent and to walk on piles of debris. Refusing to eat or drink is not part of training and can occur for other reasons. Not being afraid of people is a trait not training.

4. The Rosetta Stone (p. 18)
Reading level: 5.3

1. Which of the following best describes the main idea of the story?
   A. the war over the Rosetta Stone
   B. how hieroglyphs were figured out
   C. the British beat Napoleon
   D. the importance of the Rosetta Stone

2. Which paragraph tells the history of how and why the Rosetta Stone was made? **B**

3. In paragraph C, people had found objects with hieroglyphic writing. What did they need in order to figure out what the writing said?
   A. historians to pick out the most important objects
   B. Egyptians willing to share their language
   C. similar writing in a known language
   D. a map of the ancient Egyptian lands

Two best evidence sentences: **14, 15**

Explanation: Sentence 14 states

that you can read a passage in an unknown language by comparing a similar passage in a known language. They needed this key to decipher the hieroglyphs.

4. What is the main idea of Paragraph E?
   A. A Frenchman found the stone.
   B. It took many experts to understand the Greek writing.
   C. The Rosetta Stone helped solve a mystery.
   D. The stone had hieroglyphs and Greek.

Topic Sentence: **22**

5. How did the experts use the Rosetta Stone?

Experts compared the Greek writing with the hieroglyphs on the stone.

Best evidence sentence: **24**

Explanation: Because the stone contained similar passages in different languages, they were able to compare the unknown writing with known languages.

6. In paragraph F,
   A. What sentence supports the idea that the stone should be returned to Egypt? **28**
   B. What sentence supports the idea that the stone should stay in Britain? **29**

UNIT 2 CONCLUSIONS/INFERENCES

Lesson Answers (p. 20)

A1. *It is no longer snowing* is an **inference**

Explanation: Since the sky is clear and the sun is shining, you can infer it has stopped snowing.

B1. You probably guessed that Kenny wants to avoid Mrs. P. Which three sentences are the best evidence? **1, 2, 3 (6** also acceptable)

2. Can you tell *why* he wants to avoid her? **NO.** No evidence is given.

3. Is it a fact or an inference that Mrs. P. has stopped Kenny before? **inference**

Explanation: The story does not state that he had stopped before, but it suggests it.

4. Which three sentences are the best evidence? **1, 6, 10**

Explanation: Sentences 1 and 6 mention *this time* and sentence 10 says *caught again.*

D1. Plants need sunlight to grow.

Inference Practice Activity (p. 23)

1. Paragraph A suggests that Fred
  B. is searching for something.

  Best evidence sentence: **3**

2. In paragraph B, what do you think the sudden glimmer probably was.

  the gold coin

  Best evidence sentence: **11**

3. In sentence 12, the tale was probably about

  missing treasure (or money).

  Explanation: Fred made the statement right after he saw the gold coin.

5. "Bums in the Attic" from *The House on Mango Street*
Reading level: 3.3 (p. 24)

1. From paragraph A, you can infer that the family probably (inference)
  A. likes to go for Sunday drives together.

  B. can't afford a house on the hill.
  C. is content with their lives.
  D. thinks they'll win the lottery soon.

  Three best evidence sentences: **8, 9, 10**

  Explanation: The phrases *like the hungry, what we can't have,* and *when we win the lottery* all support the inference that they cannot afford a house on the hill.

2. From paragraph B, you can infer that the narrator (inference)
  A. spends time with people who live in the hills.
  B. feels ignored by the people in the hills.
  C. fights with the people in the hills.
  D. doesn't know any people who live in the hills.

  Which two sentences support this inference? **11, 12**

  Explanation: Sentence 11 states *they forget those of us who live too much on earth,* meaning the people who live down below. Sentence 12 supports that there is little contact between those who live in the hills and those who live below.

3. From paragraph B, you can infer that the narrator has had to put up with what three things? (inference)

  garbage, rats, and noise

  Two best evidence sentences: **13, 15**

  Explanation: Sentence 13 states that people in the hills don't have to deal with garbage or rats, suggesting that people down below do. Sentence 15 suggests that people down below hear more than just wind.

4. The narrator will let bums stay in her house so (inference)
  A. she doesn't get rats.
  B. they can sleep close to the stars.

C. **she doesn't forget where she came from.**

D. she won't be alone.

Two best evidence sentences: **16, 18**

Explanation: Sentence 16 reinforces that she will remember what her life was like before when she was in their situation. Sentence 18 says that she will offer bums housing because she has been without a house herself.

6. Secrets Revealed (p. 26)
Reading level: 3.8

1. From paragraph A, you can conclude that Lori's diary disappeared (conclusion)
   A. on the way to school.
   B. on the way home from school.
   C. **when she was away from her table during lunch.**
   D. when she looked around to see who else was near.

Three best evidence sentences: **4, 5, 6**

Explanation: Sentence 4 states that she took the diary with her to lunch. In sentence 5, she left the table with her friends. When she returned, the diary was gone.

2. You can infer that Lori didn't suspect her friends because (inference)
   A. they had already denied taking it.
   B. they hadn't had time to take it.
   C. she had asked them to watch it while she was gone.
   D. **they had left with her.**

Best evidence sentence: **5**

Explanation: Lori's friends had left the table with her.

3. In sentence 22, why did Lori walk "confidently" over to the next table? (inference)

A. **She thought she knew how to find out who stole her diary.**
B. She thought she'd see the diary there.
C. Her friends had convinced her to do it.
D. Her friends had told her who stole the diary.

Explanation: The words *I have it* reinforce the inference that she figured out a way to find out who took the diary.

4. Lori concluded that Ryan took her diary because (conclusion)

Ryan knew it was a diary even though Lori hadn't said which book she was missing.

Best evidence sentence: **29**

5. If Lori were to check for Ryan's fingerprints, in which of these places would she most likely find them? (inference)
   A. her locker
   B. **her other books**
   C. her lunch tray
   D. her purse

Best evidence sentence: **7**

Explanation: Since the diary was between books, you can infer that Ryan probably touched the other books when he took the diary.

7. Speed Skating (p. 28)
Reading level: 4.9

1. From paragraph C, you can conclude that speed skaters swing their arms to (conclusion)
   A. keep their balance.
   B. look graceful.
   C. **make themselves go faster.**
   D. prevent others from passing.

Best evidence sentence: **12**

Explanation: Sentence 12 states that their speed increases as their arms swing. There is no evidence for the other choices.

2. From sentence 13, you can infer that racers tuck their arms behind them to (inference)
   A. keep their balance.
   B. prevent slowing down.
   C. pass others safely.
   D. prevent bumping others.

   Explanation: Tucking an arm behind reduces the effect of the wind dragging on the skater. Wind dragging on a skater can slow a skater down.

3. In paragraph D, why is it harder to skate on a curve than on a straight path? (conclusion)
   A. Skaters are going faster on icy curves.
   B. Skaters are pulled to the outside by a strong force.
   C. Skaters can get dizzy on curves.
   D. Skaters don't need to crouch when skating straight.

   Best evidence sentence: **15**

   Explanation: Because centrifugal force pulls a skater to the outside, a skater has to work harder to keep moving around the curve. There is no centrifugal force on a straight path.

4. Speed skaters are most likely to make split-second decisions when they (inference)
   A. go around curves.
   B. pass the finish line.
   C. sprint off the start line.
   D. pass other skaters.

   Best evidence sentence: **22**

   Explanation: A skater must decide quickly when to pass, or he may miss

his chance. The other choices are not as likely to require that the skater make an instant decision.

5. Based on paragraphs D and E, what two things may prevent a skater from winning a race even if she or he is the fastest? (conclusion)
   1. The skater may fall.
   2. The skater may be disqualified for pushing.

   Two best evidence sentences: **20, 24**

8. The Coin (p. 30)
Reading level: 5.0

1. You can infer that the coin was valuable to Silvio because (inference)
   A. he could buy lunches for Duncan and himself.
   B. it was worth a lot of money.
   C. it was still in good condition.
   D. his grandfather gave it to him.

   Two best evidence sentences: **6, 10**

   Explanation: His grandfather had given him the coin the night before he died. The coin brought back memories of his grandfather. It had sentimental value.

2. Which two paragraphs best support the inference that Silvio regretted giving away the coin? (inference)

   Paragraphs **E** and **G**

   Explanation: In paragraph E, Silvio couldn't eat because he kept thinking about his grandfather and the coin. In G, Silvio's heart was heavy, and he felt a loss.

3. Why do you think Silvio didn't ask Duncan to pay for the food? (inference)
   A. He was hungrier than Duncan.
   B. He was embarrassed to ask Duncan again.

C. He knew Duncan was saving money for new clothes.
D. His order cost more than Duncan's.

Two best evidence sentences: **4, 11**

Explanation: Duncan had grumbled when Silvio had forgotten his wallet last time. Silvio didn't want to have to ask him to pay again.

4. From the passage, you can infer that Silvio and his grandfather (inference)
   A. disliked each other.
   B. cared about each other.
   C. spent all their time together.
   D. shared the same interests.

Three best evidence sentences: **10, 18, 19**

Explanation: All three sentences suggest the affection between Silvio and his grandfather. There is no evidence for the other choices.

5. What is the "somewhere else" that Duncan refers to in sentence 21? (inference)

He is back with his grandfather in the hospital.

Best evidence paragraph: **E**

Explanation: Silvio is remembering his last visit with his grandfather.

6. What do you think sentence 26 suggests Silvio was hungry for? (inference)
   A. another coin
   B. a chance to undo what he had done
   C. his grandfather's coin
   D. a chance to see his grandfather again

Explanation: Paragraph C describes how beautiful the coin itself was and how it brought back memories of his grandfather. Paragraph E confirms that it was the last thing his grandfather gave him.

9. Clumsy Clem (p. 32)
Reading level: 4.5

1. What can you conclude from paragraph A? (conclusion)
   A. Garth tripped his brother.
   B. Clem tripped his brother.
   C. Garth had tripped in the past.
   D. Clem had tripped in the past.

Best evidence sentence: **2**

Explanation: The words *tripped once again* are a clue that Clem had tripped over the dog before.

2. What can you infer about Clem's face from paragraph B? (inference)

He had a wart on his nose.

Best evidence sentence: **4**

Explanation: Garth calls Clem Dr. Wartnose, indicating the wart is on his nose. Also, in sentence 7, Clem is working on a wart remover that he believes will make him handsome.

3. What can you infer about the wart remover? Clem (inference)
   A. has tried making it before.
   B. just got the idea to make it.
   C. wants to give it to someone else.
   D. has never told his brothers about it.

Best evidence sentence: **8**

Explanation: Sentence 7 also suggests that he has probably made more than one version while trying to perfect it.

4. Clem was covered with four pints of what? (conclusion)

wart remover

He was opening the jar of wart remover when it spilled in sentence 12.

What was the result? **He disappeared.**

Explanation: Paragraph E supports that all of him disappeared after he spilled the remover.

5. In paragraph E, Clem's "idea" was to (inference)
  A. change the formula for the wart remover.
  B. get his brothers to help him reappear.
  C. pay his brothers back for teasing him.
  D. get his brothers to try the wart remover.

Explanation: The events in paragraphs F through J follow Clem's sudden idea. They suggest that Clem is behind his brothers' accidents.

6. Garth probably fell down because
  A. he was pushed by Clem.
  B. he was clumsy.
  C. he tripped over Ginger.
  D. he saw a ghost.

Which sentences give the best evidence?
  A. 19–22
  B. 20–25
  C. 26–27
  D. 28–31

7. Jeb probably looked like a Raggedy Ann doll because (inference)
  A. his face had red spots on it.
  B. spaghetti covered his head like yarn hair.
  C. his clothes were ragged.
  D. he could bend his body like a doll.

Two best evidence sentences: **33, 34**

Explanation: The spaghetti looked like the yarn hair on a Raggedy Ann doll.

10. From Frozen to Food, Fast
Reading level: 5.5 (p. 34)

1. To create microwaves, you can infer that a microwave oven
  A. needs more electrical pressure than what comes from the wall.
  B. needs less electrical pressure than what comes from the wall.

  C. uses electricity exactly as it comes from the wall outlet.
  D. heats faster because it uses more electricity than a regular oven.

Best evidence sentence: **11**

Explanation: Sentence 11 states that the electricity coming from the wall is boosted when you turn on the microwave oven. Therefore, you can infer that it needs more electricity.

2. You burn your mouth on the first bite of food and freeze your teeth on the insides of the food. From the article, you can infer that the food
  A. was not cooked in a regular oven.
  B. was not cooked in a microwave oven.
  C. was cooked on a stovetop.
  D. was cooked on a campfire.

Best evidence sentence: **19**

Explanation: B is the best choice because a microwave heats food evenly.

3. From paragraph E, you can tell that microwaves probably
  A. go through metal walls.
  B. cannot change direction.
  C. stop when they reach food.
  D. go in many directions.

Best evidence sentence: **15**

Explanation: Sentence 15 states that because microwaves bounce off the walls, they hit the food from different directions.

4. Is each statement a fact that is given or an inference you make? Circle **G** for given, **I** for inference
  A. A microwave is a kind of short radio wave.

  Ⓖ   I

Explanation: Sentence 13 states this information.

B. In a microwave oven, there is friction both at the edges and in the middle of the food.

G   **Ⓘ**

Explanation: You can infer this from sentences 18 and 19.

5. From the article, you can tell that molecules (inference)
   A. remain in one position.
   B. are always hot.
   C. respond to short radio waves.
   D. act like radio waves.

Two best evidence sentences: **13, 17**

Explanation: Sentence 17 states that food molecules act like microwaves. Sentence 13 tells you that microwaves are radio waves, so the food molecules act like radio waves.

11. Music for the Ages (p. 36)
Reading level: 5.8

1. From sentence 3, you can probably infer that (inference)
   A. Ashley enjoyed playing the violin.
   B. Ashley's grandmother enjoyed her playing.
   C. All people enjoy the violin.
   D. Ashley's grandmother played the violin.

Explanation: In sentence 3, the words *other older people* suggest that Ashley thought others might enjoy her music because her grandmother did.

2. Which sentences support the conclusion in sentence 1 that Ashley knows how to get things done? (conclusion)
   A. 4, 5, 6
   B. 8, 9, 10
   C. 11, 12, 13
   D. 2, 3, 4

Explanation: Sentences 8–10 give specific examples of things Ashley did to get the project going. Sentences 4–6 and 2–4 give a more general view of how Ashley started the project. Sentences 11–13 refer to the results of the project.

3. What did Ashley probably mean in sentence 13? (inference)
   A. Ashley dedicated each performance to her grandmother.
   B. Her grandmother enjoyed music.
   C. Her grandmother came to all the performances.
   D. Playing for her grandmother gave Ashley the idea for the program.

4. The name of Ashley's group probably refers to (inference)
   A. the history of music.
   B. music for young and old.
   C. the seniors.
   D. music that stays in style.

Best evidence sentence: **2**

Explanation: Ashley's goal was to bring young and old people together through the mutual enjoyment of music.

5. From paragraph C, you can conclude that (conclusion)
   A. the project is working.
   B. the project needs work.
   C. the group has failed.
   D. the group is now wealthy.

Two best evidence sentences: **16, 17**

Explanation: Both elderly patients and the high school musicians enjoy themselves.

UNIT THREE: STORY ELEMENTS

Lesson Answers (p. 38)
Conflict

B**1.** Who is the conflict between?

The conflict is between Shania and the council.

2. How will it be resolved?

Shania hopes the city council will approve her plan to use the church.

Setting

C**1.** During what historical period does the following story happen?

The time period is during the Westward Movement. (Clue: They are in covered wagons heading to Oregon.)

2. How much time goes by?

The time span is several weeks. (3)

3. How does the weather affect the story?

The heat had dried up their crops, and they were running out of money.

Mood

1. What is the mood in the following story?

There is (increasing) tension.

Character

1. What trait would you use to describe Mrs. Chan? **B** (Evidence: **4, 5, 6, 8**)

Point of View

1. From whose viewpoint is the story told?

the narrator's

2. Who is the narrator?

The narrator is probably either Scott's brother or sister. (Clue: our dad)

12. He's Got Mail (p. 42)
Reading level: 3.9

1. Which of the following best describes Ryder's problem in the beginning of the story? (plot)
   A. He may get kicked out of the lab for cheating.
   B. Emily keeps him from reading his email.
   C. Emily tells Ms. Steinmetz that he's not doing his work.
   D. He needs to write a new email.

Explanation: Paragraph A describes how Ryder had to wait to open his email because Emily interrupted him.

2. The main conflict in the story is between
   A. Trackman and Runner.
   B. Runner and Emily.
   C. Ryder and Runner.
   D. Ryder and Emily.

Explanation: Ryder thinks Emily is a pain because she is always interrupting him.

3. Ryder's problem takes an unexpected twist. How does his problem change? He realizes he
   A. hurt the girl he wanted to get to know.
   B. accidentally deleted the email he was trying to save.
   C. succeeded in getting rid of Emily for good.
   D. must tell Runner he is interested in only Emily.

Best evidence paragraph: **G**

Explanation: Ryder realizes that Emily is Runner.

4. How do you think Ryder intends to resolve his problem?

Ryder will apologize to Emily and try to be friends.

Best evidence sentence: **38**

5. Where does the story take place?

school computer lab

Two best evidence sentences: **5, 9**

6. Who is Ms. Steinmetz?
A. Emily's mom
B. the teacher
C. the principal
D. Emily's coach

Explanation: The words *in class* in sentence 9 are a clue that Ms. Steinmetz is their teacher.

7. Emily shows which of the following traits in the story? She
A. is carefree.
B. likes to argue.
C. doesn't give up.
D. is gossipy.

Best evidence sentence: **F**

Explanation: In paragraph F, Emily describes how she has tried to talk to Ryder and plans to keep trying. There is no evidence for the other choices.

13. Boat People (p. 44)
Reading level: 4.6

1. How does the crew treat the families? The crew (character)
A. was afraid of them.
B. cared about their well-being.
C. wanted them gone.
D. treated them like cargo.

Two best evidence sentences: **3, 7**

Explanation: The crew kept them below decks and did not provide enough food or water.

2. The main conflict in the story is between
A. the fishermen and the families.
B. the survivors and nature.
C. Phan and the crew.
D. the boat and the hurricane.

Explain your answer.

Phan and his sister had to survive the hurricane, the cold ocean, the lack of food, and the sharks.

Explanation: Although there seemed to be conflict between the crew and the families, the main conflict was between the survivors and the ocean. There is no evidence for C. The boat was a victim of the hurricane.

3. Phan's treatment of his sister shows that he was (character)
A. careless.
B. frightened.
C. responsible.
D. selfish.

Two best evidence sentences: **17, 18**

Explanation: In paragraph C, he rescued his sister from the boat.

4. The story reaches a crisis point when (plot)
A. there is not enough food or water.
B. the boat is destroyed.
C. the crew leaves the boat.
D. Phan and his sister swim for the rescue ship.

Explanation: B is the best choice. Phan and his sister are now in a situation where they must be rescued or they won't survive. C is important, but the refugees might still have survived without the crew. A and D are details.

5. From where is Phan telling his story? (setting)
   A. in the ocean
   B. on a small fishing boat
   C. on the rescue ship
   D. on an island

Two best evidence sentences: **1, 29**

14. Cross Country (p. 46)
Reading level: 5.2

1. Summarize the story plot.

The narrator's family is moving across country. He doesn't want to leave his friends and familiar life. But after he moves, he realizes the change is good for him.

2. Where is the end of the story set?
   A. California
   B. New York
   C. New England
   D. Washington

Best evidence sentence: **2**

3. Who is the main character?
   A. a college senior
   B. a high school senior
   C. a runaway teen
   D. a writer for a high tech company

Best evidence sentence: **6** (Also acceptable: **23**)

4. The main conflict is between

The boy and his parents

Best evidence paragraph: **B**

Explanation: The boy wants to stay in California, but his parents insist that he move.

5. How does the narrator feel about the people in the new place? (character)
   A. He feels they are not friendly.
   B. He feels they are just like him.
   C. He feels old compared to them.
   D. He feels accepted by them.

Best evidence paragraph: **E**

Explanation: Sentences 18 and 19 support that he felt he could be himself.

6. The narrator was unhappy at the beginning of the story but felt better at the end of the story. Which paragraph shows when the narrator's feelings start to change? (character, point of view)

Paragraph **D**

Explanation: He discovers the other students are friendly and like him.

7. Over what period of time does the story take place? (setting)
   A. two weeks
   B. three months
   C. twelve months
   D. two years

Best evidence sentence: **1**

15. A Run Through the Park (p. 48)
Reading level: 5.3

1. List three words from paragraph A that tell you what kind of night it is outside. (setting) Accept any three.

eerie, chilly, foggy, dreary, silent

2. Which of these things does NOT happen in the story? (plot, reading for detail)
   A. Fernanda runs through the park at night.
   B. Fernanda runs with her friends through the park.
   C. Fernanda gets lost while running in the park.
   D. Fernanda hums while she runs through the park.

3. Number the following events in the story in the order in which they actually occurred.

Fernanda

2 realizes she is lost.

1 hears stories about ghosts in the park.

4 starts sprinting.

3 sees a ghostly figure.

4. From her actions in the story, you could describe Fernanda as
   A. frightened.
   B. friendly.
   C. fearless.
   D. frustrated.

   Two best evidence paragraphs: **B, E**

   Explanation: C is best because Fernanda is willing to run alone at night in order to keep up her training. Also, Fernanda is not afraid to follow the ghostly runner. (32) Sentence 32 also contradicts A. There is not enough evidence for B or D.

5. Describe Fernanda's conflict in paragraph E.

   She doesn't know if she should follow the figure.

   How does she resolve the conflict?

   She decides to go after it.

UNIT FOUR: LITERARY DEVICES

Lesson Answers (p. 50)
Foreshadowing

1. Is the following flashback or foreshadowing? **flashback**

   In sentence 2, she *sees* Gia before the accident.

Symbolism

1. What object is used as a symbol? **crocus**

2. Explain what you think it symbolizes.

   The crocus symbolizes hope.

16. *The Face on the Milk Carton* (Excerpt) (p. 52)
Reading level: 4.3

1. Which of the following best describes the story's setting?
   A. school cafeteria
   B. study hall
   C. playground
   D. restaurant

   A is supported by paragraphs A, B, and D. There is no evidence for the other choices.

2. Which paragraphs give evidence that Janie has a conflict within herself?
   A. C, D
   B. H, K
   C. G, I
   D. M, N

   Explanation: In paragraph G, Janie can't get her hand to obey. In paragraph I, Janie wonders if she is going insane. So choice C is the best answer. Paragraphs C, D, H, K, and N contain the comments of other people, not Janie. There is no conflict in paragraph M.

3. In which paragraph does Janie relive a childhood scene? **M** (literary device)

   This is an example of
   A. mood.
   B. foreshadowing.
   C. setting.
   D. flashback.

   Explanation: Janie recalls the feelings of wearing the dress and having the braids that are pictured on the milk carton.

4. The story is told from whose point of view?
   A. the teacher's
   B. Janie's
   C. Sarah-Charlotte's
   D. Peter's

Which paragraph best supports your answer? Circle one letter.

D (F) K N

Explanation: The other choices are what Janie hears other people saying.

5. When Janie says her picture is on the carton, Sarah-Charlotte's reaction is one of (character)
   A. disbelief.
   B. sickness.
   C. agreement.
   D. fear.

Best evidence sentence: **34**

Explanation: Sarah-Charlotte says Janie is "claiming" to be kidnapped and thinks Janie is "going too far" because she wants to get out of taking a test.

6. The author uses physical changes in Janie to show her (character)
   A. growing confusion.
   B. increasing illness.
   C. lessening insanity.
   D. pleased excitement.

Give two examples of physical changes.

Accept any two: **her throat is blocked and her eyes dim** (11)**, she can't make a sound and her lips won't move** (13)**, her hand won't move** (15)**, her head hurt** (19)**, her voice sounded flat** (27, 28)

17. The Pink Umbrella (p. 54)
Reading level: 4.3

1. Yolanda could be described as (character)
   A. easily distracted.
   B. uncaring.
   C. very organized.
   D. quick thinking.

Two best evidence paragraphs: **E, F**

Explanation: Once Yolanda believes something is wrong, she acts quickly to save the little girl.

2. What clue in paragraph A foreshadows the attempted kidnapping? (literary device)

(Yolanda sees) the black sedan

Two best evidence sentences: **1, 2**

Explanation: Yolanda had noticed the black sedan cruising past before and had thought it strange.

3. How does the weather add to the mood of the story? The gray day makes the mood
   A. rainy.
   B. gloomy.
   C. exciting.
   D. boring.

Explanation: The gray, drizzly weather gives a gloomy feeling, which supports the events to follow. It also makes the little girl's umbrella stand out. Choice A is not related to mood. There is no evidence for C or D.

4. How does the author use the pink umbrella as a symbol?

The pink umbrella stands for the little girl.

Explanation: The umbrella makes Yolanda notice the little girl when she's there and when she's missing.

Also acceptable: **The pink umbrella is a contrast with the black car, like good and evil.**

Explanation: Pink is a color of innocence. Black is associated with evil.

5. What is Yolanda's conflict in the story? She is trying to
   A. get to work on time.

B. decide if something is wrong.
C. decide if she should act.
D. read the license plate.

Two best evidence sentences: **19, 24**

Explanation: C is the best choice. At first, Yolanda wonders if something is wrong, but in paragraph E she decides there is (18) and then must decide whether or not to act. Neither A nor D is a real conflict.

6. Which event helps to resolve the story?
   A. The black car starts to pull away.
   B. Yolanda hears sirens coming.
   C. The little girl falls to the sidewalk.
   D. Yolanda slams into the car.

Explanation: Yolanda decides to do something. Because she stops the car, the little girl is saved. Choice A is tempting, but the car could have simply left. Yolanda's action is the key to the story ending. Neither B nor C affects the outcome of the story.

18. Out in the Cold (p. 56)
Reading level: 3.9

1. The *main* story conflict is between
   A. Ruthie and her brother.
   B. Pa and the SnoKat.
   C. Ruthie and the SnoKat.
   D. Pa and Ruthie's brother.

   Best evidence paragraph: **E**

   Explanation: C is the best choice. The story focuses on Ruthie's struggle to get the Sno Kat going again. There is a minor conflict between Pa and Ruthie's brother, but it is resolved when Pa lets Ruthie take the SnoKat. There is no evidence for A or B.

2. Which of the following shows how Ruthie's father felt about her taking the SnoKat? (character)

A. **doubting**
B. enthusiastic
C. accepting
D. resentful

Three best evidence sentences: **6, 7, 8**

Explanation: Pa doesn't want her to go because he doesn't think she can handle it.

3. The story suggests Ruthie is capable. Which paragraph supports this inference? **H** (character)

Explanation: Ruthie shows she is capable when she figures out how to get the SnoKat moving again.

4. Which choice below best describes the setting of the story?
   A. crisp mountain day
   B. snow-covered hills
   C. cold summer day
   D. flat snowy meadow

Best evidence paragraph: **A**

5. Which paragraph contains a flashback, or description of something that happened earlier? (literary device)

Paragraph **B**

Explanation: Ruthie recalls the argument between her father and her brother.

6. Something foreshadowed Ruthie's discovery of the rock. What was it that made her think to check for a rock under the SnoKat? She (literary device)
   A. saw a rock beside the SnoKat.
   B. remembered Pa's warnings.
   C. had felt the SnoKat hit something hard before the knoll.
   D. had been thinking about rocks in a different way.

Best evidence sentence: **31**

UNIT FIVE: THEME

Lesson Answers (p. 58)

1. Which of the following is the best theme for this story?
   - A. Ballgames are only for the rich.
   - B. Sporting events are exciting.
   - C. Cheating can get you more tickets.
   - **D. Honesty is more rewarding than cheating.**

19. *Sarny* (Excerpt) (p. 60)
Reading level: 5.2

1. Which of the following best describes the theme of the story?
   - A. Running north solves many problems.
   - **B. Reading can give people knowledge of the world.**
   - C. Some people read faster than others.
   - D. Owning slaves is wrong unless you let them read.

   Explanation: Once the slaves learned to read, they also learned that slavery did not exist everywhere.

2. The men probably took longer learning to read because (reading for detail)
   - A. they didn't really want to learn.
   - B. the women were not good teachers for them.
   - C. they were slower at everything they did.
   - **D. their hard work left them tired.**

   Best evidence sentence: **6**

3. In paragraph E, reading had started to spread. Which of the following gives the best reason why this happened? (supporting detail)
   - A. Some people tried to stop it.
   - B. Other plantations heard about it.
   - **C. Each reader taught more than one person.**

   - D. Each student wanted to learn to write well.

4. What is the main idea of paragraph G?
   - **A. Slaves ran north because of what they or others read.**
   - B. In some places, no one could own another person.
   - C. No one could ever own slaves.
   - D. Slaves slowly moved north.

5. For the slave owners, what was the danger in letting slaves learn to read? The slaves would (theme support)
   - A. not have enough time to do their work.
   - B. make their masters look stupid and slow.
   - C. start reading about all the family's secrets.
   - **D. read about places where they could be free.**

   Two best evidence sentences: **12, 13**

20. Dolphin Dreams (p. 62)
Reading level: 4.6

1. Which of the following best describes the theme for this story?
   - A. Some dreams are disappointing.
   - B. If you trust people, they will take advantage of you.
   - C. Some people are luckier than others.
   - **D. Don't give up on your dreams.**

   Explanation: Throughout the story, Jane keeps working for her dream, even when she feels like quitting. The old man helps her out because he sees how determined she is to make her dream come true.

2. What is the main problem in the story?
   - A. Jane doesn't get along with her boss.
   - **B. Jane needs enough money for the program.**

C. The old man can no longer see well.

D. Jane wishes she could be with her friends.

Best evidence sentences: **4, 10**

Explanation: Jane is working and saving to study dolphins.

3. When does the story reach a crisis?
   A. Jane has two weeks to finish earning the money.
   B. Jane's boss takes $75 from her pay.
   C. Jane decides to quit her job.
   D. Jane still needs three hundred dollars.

Explanation: B is the best choice because it puts Jane further away from reaching her goal. A and D are details that support the problem. C is contradicted by sentence 17.

4. How is the problem resolved?

   The old man gives her a check.

   Best evidence sentence: **28**

   Explanation: You can infer from her reaction in paragraph E that he gave her enough money to help her reach her goal.

5. What do Jane and the old man have in common? (reading for detail)
   A. They like coffee.
   B. Their hobby is flying.
   C. They each have a dream.
   D. Their dreams became real.

   Two best evidence sentences: **5, 23**

6. Why does the old man tell Jane to follow her dreams? (supporting detail)
   A. He regretted not following his own dream.
   B. He feels too old to dream.
   C. He likes her dream better than his.

D. He wants to help dolphins.

Three best evidence sentences: **23, 24, 25**

21. The Trick (p. 64)
Reading level: 4.4

1. Which of the following is the best theme for this story?
   A. Don't judge a book by its cover.
   B. Learning is easier if you help one another.
   C. Skateboarding is for boys only.
   D. Practice makes perfect.

Explanation: Since Maria helped Randall in math, she wanted him to help her learn skateboarding, not just make fun of her. C is not the main issue in the story, although Maria and Randall tease each other about it. There is no evidence for A or D.

2. Which of the following is the main idea of paragraph A?
   A. Maria has injured herself.
   B. Pavement is not good for skateboarding.
   C. Maria is having difficulty learning a trick.
   D. Maria has given up trying to skateboard.

Explanation: Sentence 4 is the topic sentence. The other sentences are supporting details.

3. In paragraph F, what does Maria say to get Randall to see her point of view?

   She reminds him that she helped him with geometry. (or math)

4. Which of the following supports that Randall has listened to Maria in paragraph G? (supporting detail)
   A. He keeps on teasing her.
   B. He tells her how to fix what she is doing wrong.
   C. He tells her to watch what he is doing.

D. He ignores her.

Three best evidence sentences: **17, 18, 20** (Also acceptable: **21**)

Explanation: Randall starts to tease Maria again, but he stops himself and tells her what she is doing wrong instead.

5. From their dialog, you can tell that Maria and Randall (character)
   A. don't get along very well.
   B. are shy around one another.
   C. like to tease one another.
   D. don't have anything in common.

Three best evidence paragraphs: **C, D, E** (Also acceptable: **J**)

Explanation: Throughout most of their dialog, Maria and Randall laugh at one another's remarks, so you know they are teasing. It is obvious they are friends, so there is no evidence for the other choices.

UNIT SIX: VOCABULARY

Lesson Answers (p. 67)

C1. Underline the words that describe the meaning of *renovate*.

Owners of old homes often **renovate** them, <u>making them look exactly as they did when they were first built.</u>

D2. Using context clues from the sentence, what do you think the word *disheveled* means in the following sentence?

messy

Practice Activity 1

1. Which of the following words means almost the same as *equanimity*?
   A. angry mood
   B. calmness
   C. indifference
   D. anxiety

Practice Activity 2

1. Which one of the following means almost the same as *audible*?
   A. soft
   B. heard
   C. spoken
   D. high

2. Which words in the sentence help you to figure out the meaning of *audible*?

   low whisper, hear her

F1. Which one of the following words means almost the same as *introverted*?
   A. outgoing
   B. angry at everyone
   C. focused on herself
   D. excited

2. Which words are context clues?

   stopped talking to her friends, spent time alone, stared at her reflection

Practice Activity 3

1. Which of the following words means almost the same as *perturbed*?
   A. curious
   B. upset
   C. sad
   D. tired

2. Which clues in the other sentences help to support your answer?

   He wouldn't talk, he kept lighting cigarettes and pacing, he frowned

H1. What clues are you given that the word *railed* means shouted?

   The exclamation mark and the word *angry.*

22. Corporal Vinny (p. 72)
Reading level: 4.4

1. What does the word *turbulent* in sentence 2 mean?
   A. shallow
   B. deep
   C. unsettled
   D. flowing

   Which word in sentence 2 is the best context clue? **rough**

   Explanation: Since the water is rough and not calm, C is the best choice. Although choice B could fit, there is no evidence for it. Shallow water or flowing water are not as dangerous.

2. The word *agile* in sentence 3 means
   A. awkward.
   B. athletic.
   C. careful.
   D. forceful.

   Explanation: Climbing cliffs and walking narrow ledges requires skill, balance, and strength, so B is the best choice. You also have to be careful, but being careful won't give you the skill to do these tasks. The context contradicts A. There is no evidence for D.

3. In sentence 12, the word *morsel* most nearly means
   A. sniff.
   B. feel.
   C. drink.
   D. bite.

   Which word in sentence 12 is the best context clue? **tasty**

   Explanation: The word *tasty* implies that he tasted it, or took a bite. Sentence 13 also states that he tastes it.

4. In sentence 15, a long *trek* is a
   A. journey.
   B. visit.

C. escape.
D. slide.

Which phrase in the sentence is the best context clue?

back to my platoon

Explanation: In sentence 4, he also mentions that he is on a journey.

5. Which word could replace *delectable* in sentence 22?
   A. fattening
   B. delicious
   C. chocolate
   D. homemade

   Explanation: B is the best choice. Sentence 17 states the fudge is delicious. Sentence 10 also describes it as yummy. There is no evidence for the other choices.

23. Dr. Robot (p. 74)
Reading level: 5.2

1. Which word in paragraph A means almost the same as *procedure*?
   A. appendix
   B. operation
   C. robot
   D. fever

   Explanation: Sentence 6 refers to the procedure as an operation by robot. Choice B is also supported by the use of *operation* in sentence 9. There is no context to support the other choices.

2. What does the word *monitored* mean in sentence 15?
   A. gave medicine to
   B. spoke to
   C. moved tools
   D. kept track of

   Which other words in sentence 15 help give the meaning of *monitored*?

   by watching a screen

   Explanation: Only D is supported by the context.

3. Which phrase best gives the meaning of *sensitive* as used in sentence 16?
   A. able to notice small changes
   B. seen on a screen
   C. very small in size
   D. used to create signals

Explanation: You can tell from these words that choice A is best: "since his every movement had to be detected."

4. What does the word *hazardous* mean, as used in sentence 20?

   dangerous

   Which other sentence is the best context clue? **22**

   Explanation: Taking steps for safety implies that it may be dangerous.

5. As used in sentence 27, one *millisecond* is probably
   A. about an hour.
   B. more than a minute.
   C. less than a second.
   D. a million seconds.

Explanation: You can tell from sentences 25–27 that it was important for the signal to be fast enough to show immediate reactions. Therefore, anything longer than a minute wouldn't make sense. A million seconds is much longer than a minute, as are choices A and B.

6. If you do something by *remote* (in sentence 12), you probably do it
   A. by using robots.
   B. from a television.
   C. by using doctors.
   D. from a distance.

   Which sentence best supports your answer? **13**

   Explanation: The doctor and the patient were 4000 miles apart.

24. Sylvia Earle: Hero for the Ocean
Reading level: 5.8 (p. 76)

1. Which word is closest in meaning to the word *conservation*?
   A. construction
   B. damage
   C. discussion
   D. protection

   Which other sentence gives the best context clue? **4**

   Explanation: Sentence 4 explains that the ocean needs protection, so you can infer that Earle has devoted her life to its study and protection. Sentence 24 also supports that she has worked to save the ocean. Choice B is contradicted by sentence 4. Neither A nor C makes sense in the context.

2. In paragraph C, what is the best word to replace *expeditions*?
   A. tests
   B. trips
   C. vacations
   D. contests

   Explanation: An expedition is something Earle has *gone on,* which implies travel, so B or C are better choices. Since the expeditions are used to explore, B is a better choice than C.

3. Which parts of sentence 12 help explain the meaning of the word *expeditions*?
   A. gone on
   B. to explore
   C. deep parts
   D. underwater

   Explanation: Expeditions are trips taken for a definite purpose.

4. Which word can be used instead of the word *motivated* in sentence 15?
   A. prevented
   B. inspired
   C. designed
   D. forced

   Which words in sentence 15 are a context clue? **interest in** and **love for**

   Explanation: B is the best choice. None of the other choices make sense in the context.

5. Write the part of sentence 19 that explains what the word *habitats* means.

   these underwater homes

6. What is the best meaning of the word *advocate*, as used in sentence 21?
   A. photographer
   B. councilor
   C. supporter
   D. deep-sea diver

   Which other sentence gives the best context clue? **22**

   Explanation: Since her work shows her support, it makes sense that she is a supporter of the ocean. There is no evidence for the other choices.

UNIT SEVEN: FIGURATIVE LANGUAGE

Lesson Answers (p. 78)

Imagery

A1. What kind of imagery is used below?

   [1]The icy wind stung her face. [2]Tiny crystals caught in her lashes. [3]She could barely see through the blowing snow. [4]She pulled her scarf up higher.

   You can feel the wind and the cold. You can see the snow.

Simile and Metaphor

B1. Identify which sentences use simile and which sentences use metaphor and write the sentence numbers on the lines.

   Simile: **3** Metaphor: **1, 2**

C2. What kind of figurative language is used? **metaphor**

Idioms

E1. The next paragraph has two idioms. Underline the idioms then explain what you think each one means.

   [1]George thought that Clint had taken the money. [2]I told him I thought he was <u>barking up the wrong tree.</u> [3]There wasn't any proof that it was Clint, and Clint was our friend. [4]But George was <u>between a rock and a hard place.</u> [5]Either lose a friend or lose his job.

   Idiom 1 means: **going after the wrong person**

   Idiom 2 means: **in a difficult position**

Personification

F1. What is being personified in the next paragraph? **the flowers**

   The next paragraph is describing a microwave oven. Underline the examples of personification.

   [1]Sometimes <u>I'll be sitting here</u> and everything is quiet and peaceful. [2]But then somebody comes along and disturbs me. [3]First, they open my door. [4]Then they insert a big bowl of soup or a dish of spaghetti. [5]They leave it in me, close the door, and <u>poke my face a few times.</u> [6]<u>That's kind of insulting.</u>

G2. What does "poke my face" in sentence 5 mean?

   push the buttons on the front of the microwave

25. *River* (Excerpt) (p. 82)
Reading level: 5.8

1. What type of figurative language does sentence 8 contain? (simile)
   A. imagery
   B. metaphor
   C. idiom
   D. simile

   What two things are being compared in this example?

   a camera taking pictures and flashes of lightning

   Explanation: It says the lightning flashes are *like a camera taking pictures by a strobe light.*

2. What phrase is used to describe the sound the thunder made? (imagery)

   whack-crack

   Best evidence sentence: **7**

3. Which type of imagery is NOT used in sentence 16?
   A. sight
   B. smell
   C. sound
   D. feel

   Explanation: He felt and saw the bolt come roaring down the tree. He heard the loud crack of lightning.

4. How does the author use figurative language to keep the plot moving? (imagery)
   A. The sights and sounds of the storm are building up during the passage.
   B. Each paragraph contains another crash of thunder and a flash of lightning.
   C. The passage starts and ends with images of lightning.
   D. Each lightning flash shows a new action, like a series of photos.

5. What is described as a "ball of energy" in paragraph Q? (metaphor)
   A. the thunder
   B. the raw power
   C. the shelter
   D. the lightning

   Best evidence sentence: **18**

   Explanation: Sentence 18 refers to the *blueness of heat and light,* the lightning that struck Derek. This same blueness struck him in sentence 20.

6. In sentence 7, what is meant by the words "images frozen"? (idiom)

   The word *frozen* refers to the fact that each time the lightning flashes the action seems to be stopped for an instant, as if the figures are frozen.

26. Sal and Dozer Don (p. 84)
Reading level: 5.5

1. In sentence 4, what do you think the word *anomaly* means?
   A. something ordinary
   B. something awkward
   C. something unusual
   D. something mysterious

   Best evidence sentence: **3**

   Explanation: Sentence 3 tells us the football players seemed ordinary. Sentence 4 tells us there is one player that is *not* ordinary.

2. What do the words *precarious position* in sentence 9 mean?
   A. dangerous spot
   B. perfect position
   C. out of place
   D. defensive lineup

   Which sentence in paragraph B is an example of this? **10**

   (Also acceptable: **12**)

   Explanation: Sentence 10 tells us that Sal stands between the goal posts and Don. Since sentences 7 and 8 mention the destruction Don leaves on his way to a touchdown, we know this is a dangerous place to be. There is no evidence to support the other choices.

3. What does Sal compare Don to in paragraph B?

a steamroller

Best evidence sentence: **11**

Explain what this comparison means.

Dozer Don would run over and flatten the other players on his way to a touchdown.

4. Why does the author use the words *crash* and *crunch* in sentence 13?

They make sounds like a collision.

Explanation: This is a type of sound imagery.

5. What kind of figurative language is used in sentence 14?
   A. idiom
   B. metaphor
   C. simile
   D. personification

Explanation: Sal compares his body to a 7 UP® can: Sal felt his body exploding *like a 7 UP® can after it has been shaken.*

6. What does the word *disoriented* in sentence 19 mean?
   A. excited
   B. confused
   C. anxious
   D. annoyed

Which phrase in sentence 19 gives context to support the meaning?

only it was the wrong huddle

(Also acceptable: **barely managed to walk**)

27. That's Gratitude for You (p. 86)
Reading level: 5.4

1. The metaphor in paragraph A compares Mr. Grossman to a
   A. tornado.
   B. statue.
   C. wig.
   D. teacher.

   Which sentence has the metaphor? **2**

2. Write the simile used in paragraph A.

   (he was standing) **like a one-ton statue**

3. What two things are being compared in the simile given in sentence 10?

   Mr. Grossman and a wild colt

   before galloping across the floor *like a wild colt*

4. The toupee is personified in what two sentences in paragraph D?

   18, 19

   Write the phrases showing personification.

   had a mind of its own, scooted back onto the dance floor

5. The metaphor in paragraph E compares the dancers to
   A. many legs.
   B. a toupee.
   C. a centipede.
   D. a dance floor.

   Which two sentences are the best evidence? **20, 21**

   Explanation: Sentence 20 mentions the dozens of dancing legs. Sentence 21 compares these to a centipede.

6. What does it mean that Mr. Grossman's eyebrows "shot up" in sentence 26? His eyebrows (idiom)

A. flew off.
B. rose quickly.
C. slowly lifted.
D. came together.

Explanation: The word *up* tells us his eyebrows rose. Since he was surprised, they probably went up quickly. There is no context to support the other choices.

UNIT EIGHT: CAUSE AND EFFECT

Lesson Answers (p. 88)

C. Effects:

The trees were blown down. The streets were flooded. Whole houses were lifted.

D1. What was the result of letting Scooter in the house?

Scooter left a trail of muddy paw prints. Then Earl left another set.

D2. What effect did Earl and Scooter have on Shania?

They made her cry.

2. Cause: **a strike by the workers**
   Effect: **led to a safer place to work**

3. Cause: **their empty gas tank**
   Effect: **finally brought them to a stop**

4. Cause: **he was afraid to fly**
   Effect: **Jim stayed home**

5. Cause: **Mother wasn't home yet**
   Effect: **we couldn't go outside to play**

6. Cause: **Luis got up late**
   Effect: **he missed the bus**

Practice Activity (p. 92)

1. What caused the crowd to panic?

   The gorilla picked up the boy.

   Write the signal word: **because**

2. What effect does sipping Rani's soup have on Lupe?

   Her face turns bright red, her eyes water, and she gasps for air.

   Three best evidence sentences: **2, 3, 4**

28. Flash Flood (p. 94)
Reading level: 4.1

1. What caused the canyons to form? (cause)
   A. water
   B. wind
   C. hikers
   D. falling rocks

   Best evidence sentence: **5**

   Explanation: Water eroded the soft rock to form deep canyons.

2. In sentence 14, why did the hikers return to the ledge? (cause)
   A. They were still tired.
   B. They didn't want to get wet.
   C. The water had gotten deeper.
   D. There were boulders in the water.

   Two best evidence sentences: **11, 13**

   Explanation: In sentence 14, they realize that the water in the same spot is higher. A and B are contradicted by the fact that they got back in the water in 13. There is no evidence for D.

3. In paragraph C, what kept the hikers from climbing higher? (cause)
   A. the rain
   B. the ranger
   C. the deep water
   D. the steep walls

Which word is a signal word for the cause? **since**

Explanation: Sentence 17 says they could not go higher because the walls went straight up.

4. In paragraph D, why couldn't the hikers hear where the shouting was coming from? (cause)
   A. The river was too loud.
   B. The shouting was not loud enough.
   C. **The sound echoed off the canyon walls.**
   D. They were not listening hard enough.

   Best evidence sentence: **20**

5. The flood in the canyon was due to (cause)

   rain on areas upstream

   Best evidence paragraph: **E**

   Explanation: Sentence 26 states that it was continuing to rain in areas upstream. In 27, the water flowed from those areas down into the canyon.

6. What effect would this latest flood have on the canyon? It would make it (effect)
   A. **deeper and wider.**
   B. shallower and narrower.
   C. have more trees.
   D. have no water.

   Best evidence paragraph: **B**

   Explanation: The water would erode more of the soft rock away. There is no evidence for the other choices.

29. Getting the Job (p. 96)
Reading level: 4.4

1. Why are first impressions important?

   People can make up their minds about you in the first five minutes.

   Best evidence sentence: **4**

2. Being late to an interview could cause an employer to think you (effect)
   A. don't pay attention.
   B. need to get a new watch.
   C. **do not really want the job.**
   D. are a dependable person.

   Best evidence sentence: **9**

   Explanation: When you want a job, you want to make a good impression. This includes being on time.

3. Bringing important information with you will result in (effect)
   A. **making you better prepared to answer questions.**
   B. making you look organized.
   C. keeping you busy.
   D. letting you tell all about yourself.

   Best evidence sentence: **20**

   Which word in the sentence signals the effect? **so**

   Explanation: It is easier to give specific answers if you have the information available.

4. Finding out about the job ahead of time will help you to (effect)
   A. ask for a higher salary.
   B. know where else to look for a job.
   C. develop your people skills.
   D. **match your skills to the job.**

   Best evidence sentence: **25**

30. A Wad of Gum (p. 98)
Reading level: 4.3

1. Why was the narrator chewing gum in class? (cause)

   He forgot to spit it out.

   Best evidence sentence: **2**

2. Getting gum stuck in her hair caused Serena to (effect)
   A. stand up.
   B. start yelling.
   C. faint.
   D. panic.

   Best evidence sentence: **10**

   Explanation: Serena was yelling at the narrator because the gum was stuck.

3. The school officer threw Manny to the floor because (cause)
   A. he didn't like his attitude.
   B. he thought Manny was attacking Serena.
   C. he thought Manny was attacking the teacher.
   D. he wanted to stop Serena's squealing.

   Best evidence sentence: **14**

   Explanation: He saw Manny approaching Serena with the scissors, and Serena was the one who was yelling.

4. Miss Fine fainted as a result of (cause)
   A. being injured.
   B. being surprised.
   C. having a headache.
   D. all of the noise.

   Best evidence sentence: **17**

   Explanation: Miss Fine fainted because she was startled when the gum hit her. The gum wasn't heavy enough to injure her. There's no evidence for the other choices.

5. The chewing gum incident may have resulted in (effect)
   A. gum being banned from school.
   B. the narrator getting cleanup duty.
   C. the narrator being put on detention.
   D. the school being closed.

   Best evidence sentence: **22**

   Which signal words are a clue? **led to**

   Explanation: The first and last paragraphs imply that the narrator ended up scraping gum because he was the one who spit the wad of gum, which started the whole incident.

31. Animal Eyes (p. 100)
Reading level: 4.8

1. A larger eye helps an animal to see at night because it (cause)
   A. lets the animal see a wider area.
   B. increases the amount of light to the eye.
   C. can move in more directions.
   D. can make objects seem larger.

   Best evidence sentence: **3**

2. Because eyes on the sides of the head are far apart, they do not (effect)

   work together as well

   Two best evidence sentences: **10, 13**

   Explanation: Sentence 10 states that eyes that are close together focus more easily. Sentence 13 states that it is harder for eyes that are farther apart to work together. So it is, therefore, probably harder for these eyes to focus as well as eyes that are close together.

3. Because a plant-eater can see in many directions, it can (effect)
    A. find food more easily.
    B. avoid being eaten.
    C. avoid flying insects.
    D. find other plant-eaters.

Best evidence sentence: **13**

Explanation: Being able to see in all directions helps plant-eaters avoid predators.

4. An insect sees an image in pieces because (cause)
    A. each smaller eye sees separately.
    B. it looks at all the pieces at the same time.
    C. it has a kaleidoscope for an eye.
    D. each eye points in different directions.

Two best evidence sentences: **17, 18**

Explanation: A compound eye is made of many smaller eyes which can each see only part of an image.

5. Why do animals' eyes differ? (cause)

    Each animal has eyes that are adapted to fit its needs.

    Sentence 24

    Explanation: The type and position of eyes that an animal has varies according to how the animal uses its eyes. Large eyes help nocturnal animals. Eyes that are close together help predators.

32. Rubber Roads (p. 102)
Reading level: 5.5

1. What cause is given for air pollution?
    A. tires rising to the surface
    B. smog from cars
    C. tires burning
    D. using rubber tires in the road

    Best evidence sentence: **12**

2. Some buried garbage ends up above ground because it is
    A. dug up when people pull up tires.
    B. pulled along by rising tires.
    C. left over from making A-R.
    D. lighter than the tires.

Best evidence sentence: **13**

Explanation: B is the best choice because buried tires pull up other waste as they rise to the surface. There is no evidence for the other choices.

3. Which of the following is an effect of using A-R?
    A. roads made completely of rubber
    B. increased piles of old tires
    C. spread of disease by mosquitoes
    D. reduced cost of paving roads

Two best evidence sentences: **17, 18**

4. Find the cause and effect in sentence 19 and write them below.

    Cause: **rubber is flexible**

    Effect: **the road is less likely to crack** (or **the road will last longer**)

    Write the signal word: **since**

5. According to paragraph D, why does it cost less to build sound walls?

    A-R roads are not as noisy, so sound walls can be smaller.

    Which signal word is a clue to the answer? **because**

    Explanation: Because driving on A-R is not as noisy, smaller sound walls can be built, which costs less.

33. "The Path of Our Sorrow" from *Out of the Dust* (Excerpt) (p. 104)
Reading level: 3.3

1. In line 5, because wheat was selling for a high price, the farmers
   A. cooked food for people around the world.
   B. raised more cattle and sheep.
   C. joined the military.
   D. bought more land and equipment.

   Two best evidence lines: **9, 10**

   Explanation: Lines 5 and 6 stress the high price paid for wheat, which swelled their wallets so they could buy tractors and land.

2. The fact that Europe could grow its own wheat meant that
   A. the world was no longer hungry.
   B. Europe stopped buying our wheat.
   C. wheat became more valuable.
   D. Europe had more money.

   Best evidence line: **17**

3. After the war, the farmers had to grow *more* wheat in line 29 because
   A. the price of wheat went up.
   B. they needed to buy more tractors.
   C. the price of wheat was dropping.
   D. they needed to use more land.

   Two best evidence lines: **28, 30**

   Which word in line 29 is a signal word? **so**

   Explanation: Lines 28–30 explain that, because they got less money for their wheat, they had to grow more wheat to make the same amount of money they made before.

4. Put in the correct sequence the series of events that resulted in the land turning to dust.

1 They plowed up more sod.
3 The soil turned to dust.
4 The wind blew the soil away.
2 The sod dried up.

Explanation: Lines 32–40 explain that plowing up the sod dried it out because the grass that held in the water was not longer there. Without water, the soil turned to dust and blew away.

UNIT NINE: PREDICTION

Lesson Answers (p. 107)

A1. What do you think Uncle George would do if someone asked for a favor?

He would help them.

34. Mind's Eye (p. 108)
Reading level: 4.0

1. In paragraph E, if Sarah had not had the MC unit, the Too-fee would probably have
   A. used her stun stick.
   B. used her laser gun.
   C. given Sarah a tour.
   D. given Sarah directions.

   Explanation: In sentence 13, the Too-fee was reaching for her stun stick when Sarah stopped her.

2. If the Earthlings had three weeks before they needed to use the MC, they probably would have
   A. found someone else to use it.
   B. stopped the attack another way.
   C. used two weeks for testing it.
   D. found out that it was useless.

   Two best evidence sentences: **4, 5**

   Explanation: Sentences 4 and 5 tell us the device wasn't tested because they needed two weeks to test it.

3. In paragraph I, Sarah predicted that she would need extra time to control the commander. She based this

prediction on the fact that
- A. the MC unit was untested.
- B. the Too-fees were all difficult to control.
- C. he was about to attack Earth.
- **D. control was quicker with eye contact.**

Other best evidence paragraph: **F**

Explanation: Sentence 17 states the sooner Sarah made eye contact, the sooner she had control.

4. What <u>probably</u> would have happened to Earth if Sarah had not been able to use the Mind Control unit?

It would be destroyed or taken over.

Two best evidence sentences: **8, 9**

5. In sentence 45, Sarah predicts that having x-ray vision will probably help her
- **A. see the eyes of someone she wants to control.**
- B. contact the ship when she needs something.
- C. find the right people to control.
- D. see where she is going.

35. It's in the Dough (p. 110)
Reading level: 3.7

1. Predict what will happen if you make pizza using cold water.
- A. It won't make a difference.
- B. The yeast will grow more quickly.
- **C. The dough won't rise.**
- D. The dough will be more elastic.

Three best evidence sentences: **5, 9, 10**

Explanation: Yeast needs warm water to start growing. If it doesn't grow, the dough won't rise.

2. What will happen if you forget to flour the surface before kneading the dough?

The dough will stick.

Best evidence sentence: **25**

3. Predict what will happen if you leave out the sugar.
- A. The yeast won't ferment.
- **B. The dough won't rise as quickly.**
- C. The dough will be too thick.
- D. The pizza will be too salty.

Explanation: Grain has only some natural sugar. The extra sugar speeds up the growth of the yeast, giving it more food so it produces more bubbles. Leaving out the extra sugar means the dough won't rise as much.

4. Predict what happens if dough doesn't rise.
- A. It has no effect on the bread.
- **B. The bread has a heavy texture.**
- C. The dough remains sticky.
- D. The pizza will take longer to bake.

Explanation: The air bubbles give the bread a lighter texture. If bread doesn't rise, it stays flatter and heavier.

5. What will baking the dough do to the yeast? It will
- A. keep growing.
- **B. be killed.**
- C. change to sugar.
- D. burst.

Explanation: Sentence 17 states warm not hot temperatures are needed to activate the yeast. Since baking takes place at 500°, the temperature is probably too high for the yeast to survive.

6. Predict what leaving out the salt will do.
- A. The bread will rise too much.
- B. The bread may be too sweet.
- **C. The dough won't rise as much.**
- D. The yeast won't ferment.

Best evidence sentence: **13**

Explanation: Without salt, the yeast bubbles may burst, which means the dough won't rise as high.

UNIT TEN: FACT AND OPINION

Lesson Answers (p. 113)

C1. **O**

2. **exciting** The word *exciting* is a subjective term and hard to prove. The word *lots* is also hard to measure.

3. **F**

4. **The number of battle scenes can be checked.**

36. Bubblemania (p. 114)
Reading level: 5.0

1. Is sentence 3 a fact or an opinion?

   opinion

   Which word in the sentence is a clue? **best**

   Explanation: The word *best* is a value word that is hard to measure.

2. Which word in sentence 12 tells you this sentence is an opinion?

   love

   Explanation: It would be hard to prove that youngsters *love* the challenge.

3. From paragraph B, list three facts about Walter Diemer's gum.

   (Accept any three.)

   It was pink (8), **stretchy** (8), **not as sticky** (8), **sold lots** (9)

4. Label the following statements as F for fact or O for opinion.

F Bubble gum comes in a variety of shapes.
O The names of bubble gums are amusing.
F People have bubble gum contests.
O It is fun when a big bubble pops on your face.

Explanation: The facts can be proven. People may not agree the names are amusing. Not everyone may think it is fun when a bubble pops in your face.

5. Circle the letter next to the statements that are opinions.
   A. Walter Diemer was not the first person to make bubble gum.
   B. Millions of pieces of bubble gum are chewed each year.
   C. **Bubblicious® and Hubba Bubba are funny bubble gum names.**
   D. **Good bubble gum is not sticky.**

   Explanation: Both C and D ask for value judgements regarding bubble gum names and stickiness.

6. Which one of the following statements below can be proven?
   A. All bubble gum is fun.
   B. Bubble gum is silly.
   C. Bubble gum tastes better than chewing gum.
   D. **Bazooka® bubble gum came before Bubblicious®.**

   Two best evidence sentences: **25, 26**

37. Foods as Medicine (p. 116)
Reading level: 5.6

1. According to the article, which of the following sentences is a fact?
   F Oat bran helps to lower cholesterol.
   O Tea with ginseng gives you an energy boost.

   Explain your answer.

The first sentence has evidence to support it. The second sentence makes a claim that is not proven.

2. Which two of the following can help you decide if a health claim is fact or opinion?
   A. reading the fine print
   B. checking for FDA approval
   C. trying the food out yourself
   D. looking for testing

   Best evidence sentence: **12**

3. Based on the article, label the following statements as fact or opinion.
   F Quaker Oats has products with an FDA label.
   O Herbs added to foods can improve health.
   F Ginseng is an herb.
   O Functional foods are of great benefit to people.

4. Why should you be careful about believing the claims on health foods?

   Not all health foods can prove that their claims are true.

   Best evidence paragraph: **F**

UNIT ELEVEN: MIXED SKILLS

38. *Sing Down the Moon* (Excerpt)
Reading level: 3.0 (p. 118)

1. Much of the story takes place (setting)
   A. in a Spanish slave village.
   B. on the road to a white town.
   C. in a tent in a Navaho village.
   D. in a hut in a white town.

   Explanation: Paragraph B supports that the setting is a town where white people live. Sentence 21 states that she stayed in a hut. There is no evidence for the other choices.

2. From paragraph A, you can infer that the Spaniard (inference)
   A. wants to sell for a good price.
   B. sells only to white people.
   C. will sell only Indian girls.
   D. has never sold girls before.

   Explanation: The Spaniard states that he has learned that happy girls bring better prices, implying that he wants the best price.

3. The Spaniard says he has learned that Navaho girls are happy with their dogs, and that happy girls bring better prices. What later paragraph supports that he has learned this lesson? (supporting detail)

   Paragraph **I**

   Explanation: He promises to bring the woman another dog if she lets this one go. We can infer that he wants to ensure that the girl gets to keep her dog so she will stay happy.

4. In paragraph H, the old woman tries to take the dog. This is foreshadowed in which sentence? (literary device)
   A. 1
   B. 10
   C. 15
   D. 24

   Explanation: The woman was eyeing the dog in sentence 15, and the girl was afraid the woman would kill the dog for stew.

5. What did the old woman do to prevent the girls from escaping while she slept? (cause/effect)

   She lay down in front of the door.

   Explanation: Sentence 12 states that she lay down in front of the door *so* they could not open it.

6. Number the following events in correct order. (plot)
   1 The Spaniard and girls arrive at the white people's place.
   4 The narrator sees a warning in the glance of a girl who is sweeping.
   3 The woman catches the dog.
   2 The Spaniard pays the old woman.

7. In paragraph K, you can infer that the narrator thought the Indian girl (inference)
   A. enjoyed sweeping.
   B. wished she could escape.
   C. had been caught escaping.
   D. had grown up there.

   Best evidence sentence: **31**

   Explanation: The narrator felt the Indian girl was trying to tell her to run away, implying the girl wished she could, too.

39. Swim for Your Life (p. 120)
Reading level: 3.9

1. Which of the following best describes the theme of the story? (theme)
   A. All fathers should swim better than their children.
   B. Sometimes we can help those we look up to.
   C. Sometimes we have to sacrifice to do what is right.
   D. Boating near caverns is too dangerous.

   Explanation: Amanda had always looked up to her dad, who she felt could do anything. Now she had a chance to help her dad with her swimming.

2. In sentence 24, which choice could be used in place of *dispute*? (vocabulary)
   A. agree with
   B. argue against
   C. repeat
   D. explain

Explanation: In sentence 23, the father says he can't swim. In sentence 24, Amanda starts to say he can swim. Since she is arguing against what he said, choices A, B, and D make no sense.

3. What caused the cave opening to be blocked? (cause)

   an earthquake

   Two best evidence sentences: **6, 7**

   Which signal words are a clue?

   as a result

4. What do you think would have happened if Amanda did what Dad told her to in sentence 27? (prediction)

   Dad would have been killed or seriously injured by the boulders.

   Best evidence sentence: **32**

   Explanation: Since the boulders rushed at them as they jumped to the water, it is likely the father would have been injured had he remained there.

5. Paragraph I uses the words *boulders angrily rushed*. This is an example of
   A. idiom
   B. metaphor
   C. simile
   D. personification

   Explanation: In sentence 32, boulders are described as if they have the human feeling of anger.

6. Describe the conflict between the family and the boulder. (story element)

   The boulder was blocking their way to safety. They had to find a way to get past it.

   Explanation: This is an example of a conflict between man and nature. The quake caused the boulder to move, blocking the family's exit from the cavern. They had to get out of the cavern before the aftershocks struck.

7. How does Amanda resolve her conflict with her dad? She (story element)
   A. continues to argue with him.
   B. convinces him to try swimming.
   C. grabs him and pulls him under.
   D. agrees to go on without him.

Best evidence sentence: **33**

Explanation: In sentence 33, Amanda grabs him and pulls him under when they hear the boulders moving. Sentence 33 also contradicts choice A. She does try to convince him at first, but this doesn't resolve the conflict. There is no evidence for D.

8. How does the mood of the story change between paragraphs J and K? (mood)

   In paragraph J, the mood is one of fear as Amanda pulls her dad under the rock. (36) In paragraph K, the mood changes to one of joy as everyone is saved. (43 and 44)

40. The Last Will (p. 122)
Reading level: 4.2

1. Which of the following is the best theme for the story? (theme)
   A. Blood is thicker than water.
   B. Lawyers always win.
   C. Cheaters never win.
   D. Good grammar is important.

   Explanation: D is the best choice because it was bad grammar that revealed the fake will and cost them a fortune. A is contradicted by the fact that Agnes and her sons did not honor Samuel's wishes. There is no evidence for B or C.

2. Paragraph A uses a simile to describe which character? (fig. language)
   A. Samuel
   B. Sarah
   C. Agnes
   D. Mr. Goode

Write the simile used.

as sour as a pickle (sentence 5)

3. Sarah has a flashback about (literary device)
   A. Agnes and her sons.
   B. Samuel's new will.
   C. the Grammar Award.
   D. Mrs. Frump.

Two best evidence sentences: **14, 15**

Explanation: Sarah sees and hears Samuel again as he hands her a check for the award.

4. The main conflict in the story was between
   A. Sarah and Samuel.
   B. Samuel and his sister.
   C. Sarah and Agnes.
   D. Agnes and her sons.

Explanation: Agnes wants Sarah to accept a new will, but Sarah doesn't trust her.

5. In the story, Sarah felt Agnes was (character)
   A. easily upset.
   B. greedy.
   C. very pushy.
   D. friendly.

Two best evidence sentences: **7, 12**

Explanation: Choice B is supported by sentences 7 and 12. Although Sarah thought Agnes would be upset by the will, there is no evidence that she thought she was *easily* upset. D is contradicted by sentence 5. There is no evidence for C.

6. In sentence 32, what does the idiom "eyes lit up" mean? Sarah's eyes
  A. glowed like a lamp.
  B. got brighter with interest.
  C. caught fire.
  D. closed in boredom.

Explanation: When someone's eyes light up, it is with surprise or excitement. Sarah had realized the will was a fake.

7. How did Sarah conclude the will was a fake? (inference)
  A. It contained no errors.
  B. Samuel's signature was different.
  C. It contained grammar errors.
  D. Samuel didn't love his sister.

Two best evidence sentences: **33, 34**

Explanation: Sentence 16 tells us that Samuel always had perfect grammar. There are grammar errors in sentences 33 and 34. Sentence 33 should read:

...that **this** is my last will

Sentence 34 should read:

I **give** to

41. The Working Child (p. 124)
Reading level: 4.9

1. What is the main idea of the article?
  A. Children and adults worked in the textile mills.
  B. Children liked working in the mills.
  C. Children made a lot of money working in mills.
  D. Children once worked long hours in dangerous mills.

Explanation: D is the best answer. A and C are supporting details. There is no evidence for B.

2. In sentence 1, the word *textile* means
  A. fabric.
  B. factory.
  C. food.
  D. bobbin.

Which word is a good context clue? **cloth**

Explanation: Fabric is another word for cloth. A textile mill is the same as a cloth factory.

3. Why did children work in textile mills? (cause)

They worked to get money for their families.

Best evidence sentence: **3**

4. Children working in the mills had breathing problems because (cause)
  A. they breathed in cotton dust.
  B. they breathed in cold air.
  C. they didn't get enough exercise.
  D. they couldn't go to the doctor.

Best evidence sentence: **8**

Which word is a signal? **so**

5. Which one of the following sentences is an opinion?
  A. Sentence 20
  B. Sentence 21
  C. Sentence 24
  D. Sentence 25

Which word in the sentence gives a clue? **tough**

Explanation: It is a value judgement that they had a tough life.

6. Give one example of why working in a textile mill was unhealthy.

Accept any of the following:

not enough fresh air, too hot or cold, too much dust, no exercise, too little sleep

7. Based on the article, you could conclude that
   A. children liked working with their parents.
   B. adults didn't want children in the mills.
   C. children preferred school to work.
   D. adults were not paid enough to support a family.

Explanation: D is the best choice. Sentence 3 states that families needed the income from their children. There is no evidence for the other choices.

42. *Owls in the Family* (Excerpt)
Reading level: 4.6 (p. 126)

1. Paragraph A suggests that the family was (inference)
   A. pleased by Wol's arrival.
   B. expecting Wol to arrive.
   C. surprised by Wol's arrival.
   D. unaware of Wol's arrival.

Two best evidence sentences: **3, 4**

Explanation: The words *All of a sudden* in sentence 3 and *Before any of us had time to move* in sentence 4 indicate that Wol's arrival surprised them.

2. The family was unable to use the dining room for two weeks because (cause/effect)
   A. Wol's supper was still there.
   B. the room still smelled of skunk.
   C. it was too hot to eat in there.
   D. Mother wanted to wait for the rug and drapes.

Explanation: Since the skunk smell sent them choking from the room, it makes sense that it took awhile for the smell to leave. Sentence 21 also supports how strong a skunk smell can be.

3. In sentence 3, why does the author use *swooooosh* to describe Wol's arrival? (imagery)

It sounds like a bird flying.

4. Based on his behavior, you can conclude that Wol (conclusion)
   A. did not like getting dirty.
   B. wanted to please the family.
   C. was afraid of people.
   D. did not like to share.

Two best evidence sentences: **19, 20**

Explanation: Wol wanted to share his food with the family.

5. In paragraph F, the narrator gives Wol's point of view in human terms. Give one example.

Wol felt unpopular (15), **Wol's feelings were hurt** (16), **Wol was unhappy** (17), **he decided we were mad at him for not sharing** (19)

6a. What was the main problem in the story? (plot)

Wol kept bringing home the skunks he killed, which stunk up the house.

6b. How did the family resolve the problem? (resolution)

They gave Wol a tomato juice bath.

7. Write the simile used in paragraph H.

(he looked) **like a rag mop that had been dipped in ketchup**

Sentence 25

8. Which is the most likely reason that Wol never brought a skunk home again? (cause/effect, inference)
   A. He didn't want the neighbors to get mad at him.
   B. He decided to bring home squirrels instead.
   C. He didn't want another tomato juice bath.
   D. He didn't want to mess up the house.

Best evidence sentence: **26**

Explanation: The phrase *he got the idea* suggests that Wol understood that bringing home another skunk meant another bath.

43. Tiger Woods: Golfing Legend
Reading level: 5.5 (p. 128)

1. Which sentence from the passage is an opinion?
   A. Tiger has made golfing history.
   B. He is the only player to win the title three times.
   C. Tiger has used his success to encourage other young people.
   D. "He's a real inspiration for the kids."

   Explanation: Choice D is an opinion; this is one person's belief and would be difficult to evaluate.

2. From paragraphs C and D, you can infer that Tiger and his dad
   A. were good friends.
   B. shared a desire to help others.
   C. liked to work together.
   D. had nothing in common.

   Three best evidence sentences: **12, 13, 15**

   Explanation: Tiger follows his dad's beliefs. They started a foundation together to support young people.

3. Based on the article, Tiger's point of view is that
   A. it is important to encourage kids.
   B. it is best to start sports when you are young.
   C. his ethnicity is important to him.
   D. winning is everything.

   Best evidence sentence: **14**

4. In sentence 22, the word *ethnic* could be replaced with
   A. racial.
   B. athletic.
   C. golfing.
   D. educational.

   Best evidence sentence: **23**

5. Tiger made golfing history by (supporting detail)
   A. starting to play at age two.
   B. being the youngest winner of major golf events.
   C. becoming a professional golfer.
   D. being ranked number one in golf.

   Two best evidence sentences: **5, 8**

6. What is the main idea of paragraph D?
   A. Tiger's Foundation encourages young people.
   B. Tiger's dad was his role model.
   C. Tiger is a hero.
   D. Tiger started the Tiger Woods Foundation.

   Explanation: A is the best answer. Tiger started the foundation to support youth programs. He donates his time and money to encourage kids. He wants to be a role model for them. B and D are supporting details. There is no evidence for C.

44. Geocaching (p. 130)
Reading level: 5.5

1. What does the word *cache* mean?
   A. money
   B. hidden supply
   C. adventure game
   D. secret location

   Best evidence sentence: **2**

   Explanation: The word *cache* is introduced and defined in the same sentence.

2. Label the following sentences F for fact or O for opinion.

O Sentence 14
O Sentence 15
F Sentence 16
F Sentence 17

Explanation: Sentences 14 and 15 contain the words *easy* and *challenge*, which are both value words. Sentences 16 and 17 contain information that can be proven.

3. What is the main idea of the article?
A. Geocaching uses modern technology to find treasure.
B. GPS receivers make finding caches fun.
C. Finding a cache is not as fun as the adventure.
D. GPS receivers are very powerful navigation tools.

4. Is sentence 11 a topic sentence or a supporting detail?

supporting detail

Explanation: It gives specific information about what the GPS is.

5. Which sentence in paragraph C contains the main idea of the paragraph?
A. 8
B. 10
C. 12
D. 13

Explanation: Sentence 8 introduces what a GPS is. The other sentences give supporting details about what it looks like and how it is used.

6. Sentence 24 says the GPS receiver can help someone who is lost. This conclusion is based on

being able to follow a GPS path (backtrack) to the starting point

7. In which situation would you predict that a GPS receiver would be helpful?
A. navigating the Internet
B. locating meteors in space
C. scuba diving to sunken ships
D. finding a missing dog

Explanation: Choice C is correct because a GPS receiver can be used to find a premarked site, such as a sunken ship. The GPS works underwater. Choices B and C are incorrect because it is not possible to track a moving object with a GPS. There is no evidence for A.

8. Since GPS receivers transfer data over a great distance you could infer that they
A. cost a lot of money.
B. are hard to learn to use.
C. are powerful navigation tools.
D. know the exact location of a cache.

Explanation: Choice C is correct because they are small tools that can pinpoint a target anywhere in the world.

POSTTESTS (p. 132)

Fiction Posttest: "For the Love of Man" from *Call of the Wild* (Excerpt)
Reading level: 5

1. Which of the following is the best theme for the passage?
A. Only the fittest survive in the wilderness.
B. Whitewater is dangerous.
C. An animal's love can be strong.
D. All animals love people.

Explanation: Buck's love for his master sends him into the river again and again to try to save Thornton. B is a supporting detail. There is no evidence for A or D.

2. The boat turns over because
  A. Hans let go of the rope.
  B. Thornton dropped the pole.
  C. Hans stopped the boat too quickly.
  D. the boat hit the submerged rocks.

Best evidence sentence: **2**

Explanation: Sentence 2 states that Hans checked the boat too suddenly which caused the boat to turn over. There is no evidence for the other choices.

3. Which sentence in paragraph B best supports the inference that Buck is probably a dog?

Sentence **5**

Explanation: Thornton grasps Buck's tail, which tells us he is an animal. In 23, it refers to Thornton as Buck's master.

4. What does the word *rent* mean in sentence 7?
  A. leased
  B. torn
  C. bent
  D. spread

Which words in the sentence are the best context clues?

in shreds and spray

Explanation: The author is using imagery as he describes the rocks tearing the water currents to shreds. There is no context for the other choices.

5. Write the simile used to describe the rocks in paragraph B.

like the teeth of an enormous comb

Sentence 7

6. The main conflict in the story is between
  A. Buck and Thornton.
  B. Pete and Hans.
  C. Buck and the river.
  D. Hans and Thornton.

Explanation: Buck battles the whitewater rapids as he tries over and over to save Thornton and to keep himself from drowning.

7. Which best describes Buck's character in the story?
  A. frightened
  B. determined
  C. poorly trained
  D. angry

Explain your answer.

Buck is determined to save Thornton.

Explanation: B is the best choice. Buck made more than one attempt to save his master. C is contradicted by sentence 12. There is no evidence for A or D.

8. What does the word *impede* in sentence 15 mean?
  A. reverse
  B. support
  C. speed
  D. obstruct

Explanation: D is the best choice. The words *being careful* show that they don't want the line to block, or obstruct, Buck's swimming. The other choices don't make sense in the context.

9. In sentence 17, Buck concludes he should have
  A. gone straight.
  B. gone more slowly.
  C. swum faster.
  D. stayed on shore.

Best evidence sentence: **16**

Explanation: Sentence 16 states that Buck did not go straight enough into the stream. This sent him past Thornton in 17.

10. What kind of figurative language is used in sentence 23?
   A. personification
   B. idiom
   C. simile
   D. metaphor

Explanation: Sentence 23 states that his master's voice acted on Buck **like an electric shock.**

11. At what point does the story reach a crisis?
   A. Thornton is thrown into the river.
   B. Buck is carried past Thornton on his second try.
   C. Thornton lets go of Buck's tail.
   D. Thornton is clinging to a rock.

Two best evidence sentences: **14, 22**

Explanation: Sentence 14 tells us that a man can hang on in the current only for a few minutes. Buck is carried past Thornton when he tries to reach him. In sentence 22, they can tell from his voice that Thornton is in his *extremity*, meaning he is no longer able to hang on. The story has now reached a crisis point. If Buck does not go in and save him, Thornton will drown.

12. Predict what Buck will do next.

He will try again to save Thornton.

Explanation: Buck jumps up at the sound of Thornton's voice and goes back to the same launching spot. This suggests that he is ready to try again.

Nonfiction Posttest: The *Spirit of Freedom* (p. 135)
Reading level: 5.4

1. What is the main idea of the article?
   A. Steve Fossett had set many different world records.
   B. Steve Fossett overcame danger to make the first solo balloon flight around Earth.
   C. Steve Fossett tried six times to circle the globe in his hot-air balloon.
   D. Steve Fossett spent two weeks living in a balloon.

2. Fossett was involved in several endurance sports. Give one example.

Accept any of the following:

sailing, dog sledding, swimming

3. What is the main idea of paragraph B?
   A. Severe weather affected every flight.
   B. Each attempt was dangerous.
   C. Balloon flying requires skill.
   D. Fossett had to rely on others to save him.

Best evidence sentence: **6**

Explanation: Sentence 6 is the topic sentence of the paragraph. The paragraph describes some of the dangers Fossett faced on different attempts.

4. From paragraph C, you can infer that wind during a landing (inference)
   A. has no effect.
   B. provides a softer landing.
   C. can keep the balloon from deflating.
   D. may drag the balloon.

Best evidence sentence: **17**

Explanation: In this case, since the deflating device didn't work, the wind continued to drag the balloon because there was still air in it.

5. Which of the following is a supporting detail of paragraph D?
   A. The capsule's interior was small.
   B. He wore an oxygen mask only at night.
   C. The capsule was not heated.
   D. He slept forty-five minutes a day.

Best evidence sentence: **19**

Explanation: Sentence 19 states that the capsule was about the size of a closet. There is no evidence to support the other choices.

6. Since the cabin was not pressurized, Fossett (C/E)
   A. could sleep only a short time.
   B. had to wear an oxygen mask.
   C. had to fly at a lower altitude.
   D. had to keep the cabin heated.

Best evidence sentence: **22**

7. Label the following statements as fact or opinion (F/O).
   F Temperatures dropped below zero outside the capsule.
   O Fossett is the world's greatest adventurer.

8. Based on his history, you could have probably predicted that Fossett
   A. was ready to retire.
   B. would seek a new adventure.
   C. preferred sailing to ballooning.
   D. would not fly again.

Explanation: Since Fossett seems to have spent his life looking for new challenges and records to beat, you can assume he would probably have continued to do so.

GLOSSARY

character trait: tells what a person is like, such as greedy or kind

conclusion: something that must be true based on evidence that is directly stated in the story

conflict: the problem around which the action centers, usually between two characters or between a character and some outside force, such as nature. A character can have an inner conflict in which he must make a choice.

context: the other words in a sentence or sentences in a paragraph that help to define an unknown word

crisis: the point at which the problem or conflict must be solved

flashback: a shift back in time

foreshadowing: a hint from the author about what is going to happen later in the story

imagery: sensory words that describe how something looks, feels, tastes, etc. (*The leaves crackled under his feet.*)

inference: a conclusion that is suggested by the evidence in a story, but is not directly stated

main idea: what the author wants to say about the topic

metaphor: a comparison of two things which suggests one thing is the other (*He was our rock during the crisis.*)

mood: the feeling you get from a story, such as tension, fear, etc.

narrator: the person or character who is telling the story

personification: giving human qualities to nonliving things

plot: the structure of the events in a story

point of view: how the events of a story are seen

resolution: the solving of the problem or conflict in a story

sequence: the order in which the events of the story happen

setting: the time and place a story happens

simile: a comparison of two things using the word *like* or *as* (*Her arms were as solid as rocks.*)

summary: a brief review of the plot of a story

supporting details: facts that give further information about the main idea

symbolism: using an object to stand for, or symbolize, an idea or concept

theme: the underlying meaning of the story; the truth that is proven by the story

topic: the subject of a story or article

LITERATURE CITATIONS

"Day of Infamy," pg. 24
From Ginger's Diary. Copyright BZ Leonard.

"Bums in the Attic," pg. 24
From THE HOUSE ON MANGO STREET. Coypright © 1984 by Sandra Cisneros. Published by Vintage Books, a division of Random House, Inc., and in hardcover by Alfred A. Knopf in 1994. Reprinted by permission of Susan Bergholz Literary Serivces, New York. All rights reserved.

The Face on the Milk Carton, pg. 52
From THE FACE ON THE MILK CARTON by Caroline B. Cooney, copyright © 1990 by Caroline B. Cooney. Cover Art 1990 by Derek James. Used by permission of Bantam Books, a division of Random House, Inc.

Sarny, pg. 60
From SARNY by Gary Paulsen, copyright © 1997 by Gary Paulsen. Used by permission of Random House Children's Books, a division of Random House, Inc.

River, pg. 82
From RIVER by Gary Paulsen, copyright © 1991 by Gary Paulsen. Used by permission of Dell Publishing, a division of Random House, Inc.

"The Path of Our Sorrow," pg. 104
From OUT OF THE DUST by Karen Hesse. © 1997 by Karen Hesse. Reprinted by permission of Scholastic Inc.

Sing Down the Moon, pg. 118
Excerpt from SING DOWN THE MOON by Scott O'Dell. Copyright © 1970 by Scott O'Dell, renewed 1998 by Elizabeth Hall. Reprinted by permission of Houghton Mifflin Company. All rights reserved.

Owls in the Family, pg. 126
From OWLS IN THE FAMILY by Farley Mowat. Copyright © 1961 by Farley Mowat Ltd.; copyright © renewed 1989 by Farley Mowat Ltd. By permission of Little, Brown and Company (Inc.).

3 FREE SAMPLES
from our award-winning
Mind Benders® Level 5 book
and
*Building Thinking Skills®
Level 3 Verbal* book.

1. Married People

Atley, Bradley, Cursen, and Drake are the married names of Kermit, Leonard, Marlene, and Norma.

1. Drake is Bradley's sister.

2. Cursen is Atley's brother.

3. Norma and Drake are not related.

4. Kermit is a year older than Bradley.

Find the full name of each person.

Chart for Problem 1

	Kermit	Leonard	Marlene	Norma
Atley				
Bradley				
Cursen				
Drake				

HOW ALIKE ?—SELECT

Each line contains two words. Think about the ways the two are alike, then underline the sentences that are true of **both**.

A-169 deport
exile

    a. Both mean leaving a country.
    b. Both refer to native citizens.
    c. Both are usually government actions.

A-170 compare
contrast

    a. Both involve observing similarities.
    b. Both involving stressing differences.
    c. Both are useful in understanding characteristics.

A-171 language
speech

    a. Both involve words.
    b. Both can be spoken.
    c. Both are only spoken.

A-172 mumble
mutter

    a. Both refer to speech.
    b. Both sound angry.
    c. Both are barely heard.

A-173 childish
childlike

    a. Both are complimentary.
    b. Both refer to qualities typical of children.
    c. Both can be applied correctly to adults as well as children.

FOLLOWING DIRECTIONS—SELECT

Read each set of directions below, then circle the figure that correctly represents the directions.

B-10

DIRECTIONS: Draw a square. Use the top side of the square as the base of a half circle.

FIGURES:

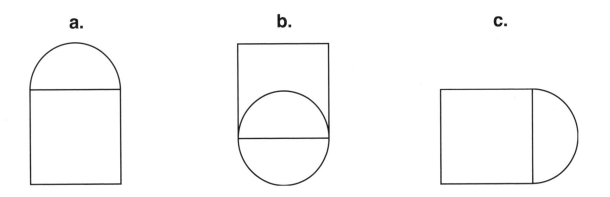

a.   b.   c.

B-11

DIRECTIONS: Draw a vertical line. Use the lines as part of a half circle and part of a triangle. The triangle should be to the left of the half circle.

FIGURES:

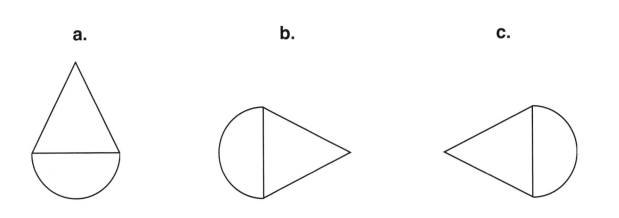

a.   b.   c.